Faith That Breathes

(for Women)

Faith That Breathes
(for Women)

REAL STORIES,
REAL FAITH

MICHAEL & TIFFANY ROSS

BARBOUR
PUBLISHING

ISBN 1-59789-241-6

Published by Barbour Publishing, Inc., P.O. Box 719, Uhrichsville, Ohio 44683 www.barbourbooks.com

Our mission is to publish and distribute inspirational products offering exceptional value and biblical encouragement to the masses.

Member of the
Evangelical Christian
Publishers Association

Printed in the United States of America.
5 4 3 2 1

For

Bonnie, Barbara, Jeanna, Ruthann,

Melba, Nancy, and Krissy

Contents

CONTRIBUTORS

Michael and Tiffany Ross would like to thank their friends who assisted with this book. These are amazing women of faith who shared stories, heartfelt advice, and much wisdom beyond their years.

Theresa "Tess" Cox—Writer and professor at Eastern Virginia Medical School in Norfolk, Virginia. Tess has recently completed her M.A. in Counseling at Regent University. She lives in a beach house on the shores of Chesapeake Bay. Her favorite authors are J. R. R. Tolkien, C. S. Lewis, Henri Nouwen, and Rich Mullins.

Vanessa S. Janusz—Computer automation and training professional in Long Island, New York. Vanessa gave her life to Jesus when she was seven years old. She has lived in six different states and has been involved in many different ministries. She attends Vineyard Christian Fellowship, where she has recently completed training in the Vineyard Leadership Institute.

Margie Younce—Program director for a nonprofit organization for children and their families in West Virginia. Along with her husband, Pete, Margie is a worship leader at New Covenant Church. She loves her family, small-town life in the mountains, her cell group, and Boston terriers.

Johanna Hulbert—*Breakaway* magazine editorial assistant in Colorado Springs, Colorado. Before joining the publishing world, She worked as a middle school teacher. Johanna is a graduate of John Brown University and is an adventure-seeker at heart. She has backpacked with friends throughout California, New Mexico, and Colorado.

Carrie Rottenborn—Writer and full-time mother in Colorado Springs, Colorado. Carrie is married and has a beautiful daughter. When she is not busy playing with her little girl, Anna, she enjoys baking anything that involves chocolate.

Katrina Forseth—Illinois state director for Child Evangelism Fellowship. Katrina holds an M.A. in Christian Education from Columbia International University and has been in full-time ministry since 1993. She loves to study the Bible and share what God has done for her through international mission trips with CEF.

voices of faith

Does your faith breathe? Is it filled with peace, love, contentment—hope? Is it renewed daily by the Source of life?

Or is your faith suffocating—weighed down by sin, entangled with legalism, and choking on religion instead of thriving on relationship?

When Jesus was on earth, He saw many religious phonies. He called them "whitewashed tombs, which look beautiful on the outside but on the inside are full of dead men's bones" (Matthew 23:27).

What's behind that face of yours? How healthy is your heart—your soul? Do others see Christ in you? Does your life read like a letter from heaven? (See 2 Corinthians 3:2–6.)

The fact that you're reading this book means you want more. You desire to stand out from the crowd—to be set apart by God. You yearn to be a woman of faith, influence, beauty, purity, courage, and purpose. But where do you begin? This devotional offers some answers.

On the pages that follow, you'll uncover the keys to a faith that breathes:

REAL FAITH

There's a difference between following Jesus and following

people who say they follow Jesus. There's a difference between fashionable, "cultural Christianity" and an authentic, life-changing relationship with the God of the universe.

A faith that breathes involves firsthand fellowship with Jesus Christ—which is always more invigorating and dependable than secondhand religion.

Anytime you put your faith in other people, you're bound to be disappointed. That's because people—even those churched variety—sometimes get jealous, lose their temper, and focus on the surface instead of what's inside. Because they're sinners—just like we are—they even do things they know are wrong.

But there's one person who is absolutely authentic; someone you can always count on. Jesus Christ. In the days ahead, you'll look at Him, read about Him, and study about Him. You'll see that Jesus embodies genuine Christianity.

REAL JOURNEY

By the time you're, say, seventy, what would you like your relationship with God to be like? Will you have been faithful to God? Will you have forgotten Him? What will you have accomplished for God or for yourself? What will your most important relationships look like? Whom will you have significantly influenced for God's kingdom? Will the temptations, hassles, and doubts you struggled with have brought you closer to God or pushed Him away? Will others say that you "fought the good fight. . .finished the race. . .[and] kept the faith" (2 Timothy 4:7)?

On the pages that follow, you'll read about the real journeys of people just like you. They'll offer some clues that will help you look back on your life with a sigh of relief—not a sigh of regret.

REAL GROWTH

Don't hold back. Take a cleansing breath—meditate on God's Word. Then exhale: Tell Him about all the junk you want Him to clean out of your life. Tell Him you want to stop being a phony, lukewarm Christian—and to start being genuine like His Son. Remember this: "If we confess our sins, he is faithful and just and will forgive us our sins and purify us from all unrighteousness" (1 John 1:9). Confess your hypocrisy as often as you become aware of it. The Bible's truth never wears out.

PURE, LIFE-GIVING OXYGEN!

This book is designed to help you discover a *Faith That Breathes*.

Is this a devotional? Is it a small group study guide? Actually, it's all that and more! Inside you'll find:

- daily Scripture readings and devotionals that unlock biblical truth, along with tips on how to grow in your faith.

- engaging real-life stories from women who also desire an authentic, living, breathing faith.

- helpful insights and **Real Journey** stories from contemporary Christian artists.

Study the Bible, pray, and read this resource from cover to cover for the next forty-two days—especially before launching into a Christian service project or heading out on a summer mission trip—and you'll experience a renewed spiritual life.

The more you seek a *Faith That Breaths*, the more you will find that Christ lives His life through you.

a woman of faith

change: it's inevitable

"In the beginning you laid the foundations of the earth,
and the heavens are the work of your hands. They will perish,
but you remain; they will all wear out like a garment.
Like clothing you will change them and they will be discarded.
But you remain the same, and your years will never end.
The children of your servants will live in your presence;
their descendants will be established before you."

—PSALM 102:25–28

Life. It's filled with wonder and discovery, and it's defined by change—as you probably know all too well. Yet for most women, change is both a comfort and a curse.

As a young teen, I (Vanessa) remember how intrigued I was by all the older girls racing through the halls at school—each so unique and varied in appearance and stature. I couldn't help wondering how I was going to turn out. Who was I becoming? What challenges lay ahead for me? How would I handle the many changes I'd encounter as a woman? Most important: How would I fit into that vast sea of faces?

I'll never forget finding one of those books that lists hundreds of different names along with their meanings.

Some names meant "gift of God" or "mighty warrior" or "blessed of God."

Cool! I thought. *I wonder what my name means?*

I quickly flipped through the pages, searching for my "identity"—convinced that I was about to uncover an eye-opening clue about the woman I was destined to be.

My fingers slid through the Vs, then stopped. *Vanessa.* Bursting with excitement, I began to read: "Butterfly."

Butterfly?

My jaw dropped and I slumped back in my chair. *That's it? This can't be right! I'm a butterfly?*

Yet there it was in stark, black print. The book explained that the name *Vanessa* was Greek for the word *butterfly.* And that was all it said—nothing more. I was stunned.

Why didn't my name mean something grand, something larger than life—something filled with splendor? Why didn't my name speak of a woman who is connected to God in some special way?

Not long after that humbling experience, I spotted a butterfly one summer afternoon flitting around in my backyard. I paused and watched it carefully. "So, this is me," I reminded myself.

It certainly was a beautiful creature, yet it was still just an insect! It wasn't all that spectacular. It wasn't even significant enough to change the world. Frankly, it wasn't anything to get excited about.

But as the weeks passed by, I began to learn more

about these fluttery creatures. Gradually, I became fascinated by what I'd read—especially by all the changes that take place during a butterfly's lifetime. It comes into the world rather ugly and pitiful looking—a caterpillar!—certainly not something you'd want to touch. Then it changes. Stage by stage, it is transformed into an entirely different creature, eventually becoming so beautiful that it graces the heart of nearly everyone who sets eyes on it.

And, believe it or not, butterflies are strong. Despite their fragile appearance, monarch butterflies migrate every year from Canada to South America—and then back again. (I can't even imagine traveling that far on foot!)

The truth is, the life of a butterfly means *change*. Constant change. Just as in my own life—and in the life of every woman.

• • •

As we begin our journey into womanhood, we're often unsure of who we'll become, how we'll look, what paths we'll follow. Yet somewhere between youth and maturity, we begin to realize that life is full of uncertainty. *Who will I become today, tomorrow, next week—next year?* We identify, ever so slowly, the changes taking place in our lives, shaped by internal and external forces. Men are often lauded for their courage, but it also takes a lot of courage to be a woman in our ever-changing and uncertain world.

Here's something wonderful to consider: As

women, we have an opportunity to practice our faith in a mighty way. The faith we need to step around every new corner—nearly always uncertain of who He is shaping us into—is a rather enormous character trait, isn't it? This alone should instill us with confidence.

Above all, we must hold the hand of the One who loves us and accepts us for who we are as we face life's challenges and uncertainties.

With Jesus by our side, each new day brings a new adventure—a journey we can embark upon without fear. The Lord's voice whispers confidence and truth to us along the way. He offers a strong arm that we can lean on. He gives us a shoulder we can cry on. He extends a hand that guides us through each stormy sea and every quiet meadow in life. He is the lover of our souls.

Despite all the fierce storms I have weathered in my life—the disappointments, the trials, the hurts—I will never regret a single day that I have walked with Jesus, those priceless moments when I have held the hand of my Savior. Somehow He makes the bitterest slices of life so sweet.

Over the years, I have encountered many changes—some I have welcomed; others I have dreaded. And, like it or not, for better or worse, change has shaped my life. But through it all, I've learned that I don't have to fear change as long as I stay close to Jesus. I can accept—I can actually appreciate!—what He is accomplishing in my life. *Everything* is in His sturdy and capable hands.

Sometimes change is hard. Come to think of it, the

butterfly that struggles to emerge from its tiny chrysalis would no doubt agree. But I have learned to walk with Jesus and say, "Bring it on!" I have learned to seek and embrace change on a daily basis.

If it's true that "the only thing constant is change," then I would encourage every woman to pursue those changes that will lead her upward and onward, toward goodness and truth, and closer to Jesus.

A FAITH THAT BREATHES

. . .knows that if our security is in the world, we're in trouble. The world will always change, and the things we hold so tightly today may fall out of our grasp tomorrow.

. . .is confident that the Lord remains the same—yesterday, today, tomorrow, forever! He promises to be our guide, our stability, our hope.

. . .welcomes the changes that God sends our way. Strive to welcome change with open arms. Embrace it as the priceless gift that it is. Learn to stand hand in hand with Jesus and declare, "Bring it on!"

NICOLE C. MULLEN
God Is Faithful

Change certainly defines my life. Holding down a family and a music career involves more challenges, surprises, and changes than any person could ever want. Yet through it all, I've learned to lean on Jesus Christ—the one Person who never changes—for comfort and direction.

I grew up in a Christian home in Cincinnati, Ohio, listening to Amy Grant—and imagining one day having my own recording career. I'll never forget what my sister once told me. She came to me one morning and said, "I had a dream. In it, you were on stage singing with Amy."

My response: "Yeah, right—whatever!" Then I sort of put it out of my mind. But a few years later, my sister's dream became reality. After I signed my first recording deal and released my first album, *Don't Let Me Go,* I received a phone call from—guess who? That's right—Amy Grant's managers!

They asked if I'd audition for her Heart in Motion tour. So I did, and they liked me—and the rest, as they say, is history. My life began to change in dramatic ways. Not only did I get to tour with my favorite singer—I was a backup vocalist and choreographer—but my own music career really began to take off.

Many years later, my greatest goal as an artist is something that has never changed: I want people to walk away after my concerts feeling excited about their faith. I want them to see the world from a new perspective—God's perspective.

I want people to see that I have hurts and struggles, too. But I've learned to pick up and move on. Through it all, God is always faithful.

pursuing Christ

> "I am the good shepherd;
> I know my sheep and my sheep know me—
> just as the Father knows me and I know the Father—
> and I lay down my life for the sheep."
>
> —JOHN 10:14–15

I (Tess) grew up in a very conservative church. It was a small country congregation where women wore long skirts and long hair, the pastor preached long sermons, and the Sunday school classes were devoted to a long list of rules on how to attain personal holiness.

I was taught that if I stayed in church, followed the rules, and didn't do the "don'ts," then I would experience holiness and the fullness of Christ. In other words, I'd be acceptable to God.

I did my best to always be a "good girl," and I was very proud of the fact that I was also a good Christian. *God must like me very, very much,* I convinced myself. I thought I had Him in my back pocket and the entire Christian life figured out by the time I was fifteen.

Then it happened. I lost Him. I completely lost track of Jesus.

• • •

One day when I was in college, I spent time in reflection,

examining my heart, yet the Lord seemed to be nowhere near me. I searched and searched, I prayed and prayed. But the deep coolness, the placid emptiness of my heart remained. It wasn't just that I couldn't feel God's presence. I soon realized that I couldn't really feel *anything*. I didn't laugh or cry or feel sad or happy. I just *was*—and I felt very alone.

For four years I called out to God to come back to me. I did everything I could to get His attention. I did nearly everything on the list of spiritual "do's." I went to church as often as possible and even sang in the choir. But all the while my heart felt dead and very much afraid. I couldn't figure out what I had done to deserve this kind of abandonment.

Then, one balmy Florida night—I lived in Jacksonville at the time—I heard a song by Keith Green that caught me by surprise. I was bent over the sink, washing dishes in my little apartment, as the lyrics blasted through my radio: "You pride yourself with all your searching, but why are you searching in the dark? You won't learn a thing until you soften your heart!"

Those convicting words pierced my heart. I instantly realized that I had been searching for a "God of rules"—a God whose love and favor was dependent on something He required—no, *demanded*—in return. In all honesty, I was looking for a God who didn't really exist. I was searching in the dark.

As my tears dripped into the dishwater, I cried out, "Show me how to love You! Show me how to soften my heart toward You. Change me!" I wept and wept as four years of numbness began to melt away.

In the weeks that followed, I began to experience a closer relationship with Jesus. I gradually came to understand the principle that would guide my relationship with God for the next twenty years: "I need to fall in love with Jesus!"

I realized that I must pursue Him as I would pursue the heart of my husband. I must pursue Him as my closest companion and best friend in life. I must put all else aside to be with Him. He must be the priority of my heart, even while I attend to the everyday business of life. I must pursue His heart, His passions, His character, and His truth for my life. I must look at Him with love and open my heart to His wooing.

So I began to pursue Jesus. Every moment of every day I called out to Him—reaching out my spirit to touch His and tuning my spiritual ears to hear His voice. Each day as I arrived home, I would walk over to the fireplace and wait. It was a symbolic gesture, signifying that I wanted the fire of His heart and His love inside me. I would wait in the quiet for His presence, and He would come and speak softly and sweetly to my heart. He would remind me of the day, show me my own heart, and reveal my inner being to me. Gently, He began to heal and coax and teach and love me into His image.

As I spent time with Jesus, pursuing His heart, my times of private communion were heightened. I began to listen to Christian albums and to sing to the Lord a new song as commanded in the Scriptures.

Spontaneous songs of sweet love and adoration would come out of my heart to Jesus. I began to see Him as my King and my Lord, my Husband, Protector, and Provider. Jesus became all to me. His presence was sweet and powerful.

I began to see visions and pictures of His will for my life as He prepared my heart for something that was about to happen. Sometimes He would give me a vision of how He was transforming my spirit—or a glimpse of something He was doing in the world around me. He added wisdom and light to my often darkened understanding.

Are you ready to stop searching in the dark? Are you yearning to fall in love with Jesus and begin pursuing Him with all your heart?

A FAITH THAT BREATHES

. . .*connects daily with the Source.* When I was younger, I used to love watching the original *Star Trek* series. In one particular episode, the crew of the starship *Enterprise* arrived on a planet where a young woman was found to be living all alone. Seeing that it was a barren planet, with no visible resources, the crew asked her how she survived. She told them that she was looked after by the Caretaker. Each day, she would stand in a certain place and invite the Caretaker to come. And each time, this beautiful, sparkling cloud would descend upon her from the atmosphere and envelop her with its presence and life-giving energy.

. . .*experiences the raging fury of God's love.* I have seen His heart, His mind, and His incredible passion. I have been enveloped in the cloud of His presence. He surrounds me and covers me. His presence saturates and bathes me. And His love and truth and purity wash me and sanctify and transform me. Always from these moments come repentance, release, and fire.

. . .*pursues Christ with outstretched arms.* In the time you've set aside today for devotions, open your arms and run to Jesus. Pursue your Savior, completely unguarded and vulnerable to His piercing truth and relentless love for you. He is waiting to share with you His passion. He says to you, "The water I give. . .will become in [you] a spring of water welling up to eternal life" (John 4:14). Jesus wants to saturate you with His refreshing Spirit. He desires to wash you with the water of His Word and nourish you with His unconditional love. Draw near to Him. Jesus will hold you up in His strong arms.

GINNY OWENS
The Pursuit of Christ Involves Struggle

I can't think of a single Christian who hasn't struggled in one way or another. It's simply a part of life and something we'll always face, regardless of how old we are. Yet as we face trials in life, what happens? Fear begins to take over. It seems as if struggle and fear go hand in hand. In fact, fear is one of Satan's favorite tools to use against us.

But here's the good news: God tells us—from the beginning of the Bible to the end—that He has conquered fear and has overcome the trials and tribulations of this world. We are no longer slaves to them. As His children, we are free!

How?

The Lord is faithful, and He can be trusted. Remind yourself of these truths every day. Above all, pray through your circumstances, and do all you can to fight fear. Here's something that has helped me: I like to memorize Scripture.

It's amazing how, during the hard moments, a certain Bible verse can pop into your head. The Lord will use it to strengthen you and to fight Satan. Try memorizing Scripture that tells how God has conquered fear and has overcome the world, such as this one: "This is love for God: to obey his commands. And his commands are not burdensome, for everyone born of God overcomes the world. This is the victory that has overcome the world, even our faith. Who is it that overcomes the world? Only he who believes that Jesus is the Son of God" (1 John 5:3–5).

When struggles hit and fear consumes, do your best to

stay focused and disciplined. And never stop trusting God. It is my faith in Jesus and my trust in Him that has given me the confidence to say to my heavenly Father, "I will walk through the valley. . .if You want me to."

DAY THREE

Holy Spirit encounter

When the day of Pentecost came, they were all together in one
place. Suddenly a sound like the blowing of a violent wind
came from heaven and filled the whole house where they
were sitting. They saw what seemed to be tongues of fire
that separated and came to rest on each of them. All of
them were filled with the Holy Spirit and began to
speak in other tongues as the Spirit enabled them.

—ACTS 2:1–4

It's easy to get lost. Sometimes in the whirlwind of emotions, relationships, and duties of our lives, we lose our
bearings. Suddenly, our spiritual compass no longer
points toward true north.

Here's something amazing to consider: *True north*—
the magnetic center of our revolving planet—is not the
same north that we would assume when looking at a
map. Why? It's because our spinning little world is tilted
slightly askew on its axis. That tiny little tilt of about four
degrees is what causes us to experience the seasons.

It's a lot like our spiritual lives, isn't it? Our tiny little
worlds, knocked askew by original sin, spin completely
out of our control—always bringing new seasons to our

lives. And, just as in nature we adapt to the seasons, we must also meet each spiritual season as it comes, dealing with heat and cold, drought and flood—whatever circumstances we encounter. As we continue to spin, tilted under the burden of sin and doubt, how can we maintain our orientation to true north?

• • •

On maps of the ancient world, cartographers always print an arrow pointing to true north. Even if there is no east, west, or south enjoined to the symbol, with the invaluable assistance of a compass, an arrow and the large **N** indicate the right direction to keep you oriented.

When we come to Christ, He places a compass in our hearts. " 'If you love me, you will obey what I command. And I will ask the Father, and he will give you another Counselor to be with you forever—the Spirit of truth. The world cannot accept him, because it neither sees him nor knows him. But you know him, for he lives with you and will be in you. I will not leave you as orphans; I will come to you' " (John 14:15–18).

Jesus changes us with the presence of His Holy Spirit—the Counselor who works deep inside us as our Comforter, Compass, and Guide. He constantly points us toward His heart—our true north.

We also use the map of His living Word to prayerfully chart our course and seek our final destination: His character and likeness.

Count on this: The presence of the Holy Spirit will always keep pointing us toward the heart of Jesus. When our lives seem to spin recklessly out of control, it is more important than ever to immerse ourselves in

a woman of faith —

the magnetism of His presence, the overwhelming pull of His love and His Word.

It is possible to lose sight of our true north. The storms of life throw us off course, and we ignore God's internal compass to focus on righting ourselves. How can we reconnect with the Holy Spirit? More importantly, what can we do to maintain that connection daily?

A FAITH THAT BREATHES

. . .*seeks Him with a focused vision.* God says, " 'You will seek me and find me when you seek me with all your heart' " (Jeremiah 29:13). The Holy Spirit is not "out there" somewhere, waiting for us to have just the right combination of perfection and success in our spiritual lives before He'll reveal Himself to us. To believe this is deception! The Holy Spirit resides *inside* us. How can we see inside ourselves? By becoming quiet for a few seconds and focusing on who we are in Him in this moment and who He is—the character of God. Remember what Jesus did for us on the cross. We must see ourselves as valued and redeemed by Him.

. . .*seeks Him through prayer.* " 'Ask and it will be given to you,' " the Lord reminds us. " 'Seek and you will find; knock and the door will be opened to you' " (Matthew 7:7). Consider praying this prayer to God: "Father in heaven, I am lost and do not know my way in this world. Show me the way, Lord Jesus. Reveal Yourself to me, Holy Spirit. I open the door of my heart to You now. Show me Your face and help me to focus on You and hear Your voice clearly. Help me to keep my walk with You simple and uncomplicated by doubts. Teach me to trust You and hear You as a little child. Help me to know You more and more. Help me to know who I am and what I am capable of in the knowledge of You. I wait on You and depend on You for every part of my life."

. . .*seeks Him as a lover.* Remember that we are His beautiful Bride. Every man who loves his wife will make love to her and cherish her, protect and champion her as his own. The Holy Spirit is the presence with us, causing us to become one with Him in spirit—even before we meet Him face-to-face. He joins Himself with us in a sacred betrothal, a sacred union.

According to Scripture, "A man shall leave his father and mother and be joined to his wife, and they shall become one flesh" (Genesis 2:24 NKJV). Likewise, the great lover of our soul has joined Himself to us. He is creating us from the inside out into that image (or Body) of "oneness" where our unity with His Holy Spirit causes us to be made over into His likeness. Love transforms us. And on that day when we shall see Him face-to-face, and our wedding supper is convened, all He will see is His precious Bride—holy, righteous, adorned in spotless raiment, and blameless before Him. How so? The Holy Spirit will have done His holy work by washing us with the water of the Word and baptizing us in His presence so that we are saturated with Him— clothed in white raiment.

. . .*seeks Him minute by minute—despite busy schedules.* Take a few moments every day, even if it's just for a few seconds, to quietly soak in the presence of the Holy Spirit. This will bring both refreshment and His creative, purifying presence into the moment with you. As He promised, He will never leave you nor forsake you. Seek Him daily—your true north.

MARGARET BECKER

Supernatural Wonder

I'll never forget an experience I had at one of my concerts. This happened many years ago, right after the release of my *Just Come In* CD.

A girl came up to me after the show and said she had played the song "I Don't Want to Be without You" for her older sister, who was going through some horrible stuff. Her sister committed her life to the Lord as a result of the song. Two weeks later, she was killed in a car accident.

Her story touched my heart. I couldn't stop thanking God for using me for His eternal purpose. I realized how important it is to always stay tuned into the Holy Spirit.

Through the years, I've been blessed with other stories from people who listen to my music. I also remember a thirteen-year-old girl who shared her story with me. As we talked, tears rolled down her cheeks. She believed her older brother was on drugs because of the friends he was hanging out with, and it was causing a lot of problems in her family. She wanted to help him but didn't know how. After all, she was the younger sister.

We prayed together, and I suggested that she should express her love for him and let him know that even though she's young, she'd like to help in any way she could. I vividly remember her crying and looking determinedly at me, saying, "That's what I'm going to do. Tonight, I'm going to tell him."

I knew it would be difficult for her to talk to her older brother. Yet I could see how deeply she cared for her brother— she was broken for him. I was convinced that the Holy Spirit would give her the right words. As she left, I knew that God was going to accomplish something amazing through her tender faith.

unstoppable worship

Praise the LORD. Praise God in his sanctuary; praise him

in his mighty heavens. Praise him for his acts of power;

praise him for his surpassing greatness. Praise him with

the sounding of the trumpet, praise him with the harp and

lyre, praise him with tambourine and dancing, praise him

with the strings and flute, praise him with the clash of cym-

bals, praise him with resounding cymbals. Let everything

that has breath praise the LORD. Praise the LORD.

—PSALM 150:1–6

In every church there is a liturgy for worship—whether this means three hymns and a morning prayer or the full Eucharistic litany. It all depends upon your tradition. Actually, the liturgy of the Christian church was derived from the original Jewish liturgy of the ancient church fathers and apostles. Whatever the tradition, our worship today ties together those ancient rites with the "liturgy of heaven."

What is the liturgy of heaven? Revelation tells us that those who have gone before us with the angels stand continually in God's presence crying, " 'Holy, holy, holy is the Lord God Almighty, who was, and is, and is to come' " (Revelation 4:8).

When we worship today, we are compelled as citizens of heaven to cry "Holy!" The worship in heaven is continual and unstoppable. Why? Because of who God is. He is the Center, the Light, and the Foundation of heaven. He is Holy and Almighty. He is Love.

We cry out for the heart of our first Love—the first Love of humanity—our first Friend and Caregiver. We seek Him from the moment of our birth to the moment of our passage from this life into the next. Every breath and spoken word is a part of the liturgy of our lives.

As daughters of heaven, this liturgy is played out as we make decisions, relate to others, and surrender our true selves to the Holy Spirit. The Holy Spirit within us is in continual communion with the Father and the Son. Therefore, as we surrender our hearts and spirits to His movement and flow, we become more and more engaged in that Holy communion with Him.

Communion may be seen as part of the Eucharist with which we participate during a worship service. But *communion* also means *fellowship*—known as *koinonia* to the Greeks. Our *koinonia* with Christ is strengthened as we delve into the Word of God and partake of the Bread of His Body. As we keep our eyes focused on His face and our ears tuned to His still, small voice, our communion with Him deepens and our spirit finds a path of connection. This creates a continual conduit for His presence in the everyday moments of our lives. Our spirits become tuned to the liturgy of heaven and a song rises from deep within us, crying, "I love You, Lord, and I lift my voice to worship You. O, my soul, rejoice!"

A FAITH THAT BREATHES

. . . is tuned in to unstoppable worship. Get this: We are the temple of the Holy Spirit—"this treasure in jars of clay" (2 Corinthians 4:7). The liturgy of heaven is meant to be carried out inside our earthly temples. Worship Him. We experience holy communion *(relationship)* with Jesus, our High Priest. Unstoppable *koinonia.*

. . . worships God day by day, moment by moment. In John 4:23–24 Jesus tells us: " 'Yet a time is coming and has now come when the true worshipers will worship the Father in spirit and truth, for they are the kind of worshipers the Father seeks. God is spirit, and his worshipers must worship in spirit and in truth.' " In other words, the place of worship is irrelevant, because true worship must be in keeping with God's nature, which is spirit. Above all, our heavenly Father has no use for empty ritual or worthless words that bounce off the walls of man-made temples. *We* are His temples. He wants from us real worship that flows from our hearts—the kind that is spontaneous, unceasing, and filled with delight. He desires true worshipers: those who acknowledge Him as Lord and Savior with both their lips *and* their souls.

. . . partakes in the liturgy of heaven. Let us draw near boldly to the altar of His grace, which is within our hearts. Let us partake of the liturgy of heaven.

REBECCA ST. JAMES
The Worship Revolution and You

It's everywhere—filling the airwaves, selling out concerts, topping CD collections. All over the world, people are plugging in to worship music. And that excites me! But here's my challenge: Make worship your Christian lifestyle, not just your music choice.

I've come to realize that worshiping God is an interactive experience—whether it's through music or prayer. "Come near to God and he will come near to you" (James 4:8). It's both private and public. It involves our hearts and our heads. And as we linger in God's presence, praising Him, we become transformed. Worship actually builds us into stronger Christians.

So, how's your worship life? Have you made it a priority? Or do you feel as if your Christian walk is shallow and ineffective?

I believe worship is one of the greatest things we can do here on earth. It's our human Christian calling; it's what we're created to do. I love worship. God created us out of His desire for fellowship. He wants us to choose to worship Him. He didn't make us robots. Instead, He gave us a choice. Worship is an essential ingredient in the Christian life.

So, how should you do it? Keep worship natural—never forced. If you're having trouble getting started, think about His blessings and who He is. Just praise Him for His faithfulness and His love that He's shown you. Praise Him for His creation. Look at the world around you and praise Him for it. I sometimes sing a worship song to Him. Some of the most amazing times in my life have been experienced during worship.

daily bread

" 'Our Father in heaven, hallowed be your name,

your kingdom come, your will be done on earth

as it is in heaven. Give us today our daily bread.

Forgive us our debts, as we also have forgiven our debtors.

And lead us not into temptation,

but deliver us from the evil one.' "

—MATTHEW 6:9-13

Early each morning, even before the rooster crows and the sun peeks over the mountains, the Friedman family goes to work. They enter their storefront business in Lewisburg, West Virginia—a popular local hangout simply called The Bakery—and begin their daily routine of baking bread.

Eggs, oil, flour, yeast, and milk are hand mixed in large bowls. Then a whole bunch of other ingredients—such as honey, cheese, oats, sun-dried tomatoes, and flax seed—are added to the bowls of dough to make an assortment of unique and flavorful breads. The family recipes, passed down for generations, are seemingly endless. In fact, The Bakery's menu of delectable breads varies each day.

Sticky lumps of dough are turned out on floured

wooden boards and are kneaded and dropped in greased pans. As the dough gently rises, overflowing the sides of the pans, a glaze of beaten egg whites is lightly brushed on top of each loaf. Then comes the final step: The pans are placed into hot brick ovens and are baked until the bread turns a perfect golden brown.

Can you smell the aroma? Nobody in Lewisburg can miss it! The heavenly scent of hot baking bread drifts through the streets, enticing people from all over town. By daybreak, a line of hungry West Virginians forms in front of The Bakery's wooden screen door. They wait their turn to squeeze into the tiny store, anticipating the opportunity to sample and choose from countless varieties of bread. "I could make a meal out of the bread alone!" says a happy customer.

Handwritten cards that list the ingredients are taped on the racks above each loaf of bread. The Friedman family—still wearing their bakery aprons dusted with flour—offer customers samples of their mouth-watering creations and make recommendations on which loaf goes well with a specific meal. Customers bring their selections to the counter, some purchasing bread to share with coworkers for lunch and others requesting that their loaves be wrapped up in brown paper for dinner. Everyone leaves the store smiling and toting trophies in paper sacks.

Regular customers know there is no need to buy more than they can use in a day, because every morning there will be more wonderful, aromatic, fresh bread baking in The Bakery's oven. The Friedman family tradition of baking bread has continued faithfully every day for the past fifty years.

• • •

They broke bread in their homes
and ate together with glad and sincere hearts,
praising God and enjoying the favor of all the people.

—ACTS 2:46–47

Warm bread is comforting and satisfying, isn't it? We can joyfully break bread with friends around a dinner table or in the workplace lunchroom. We can enjoy it alone with tea and jam. We can slice it and make cinnamon toast for our children. We can give loaves as gifts to friends who need encouragement.

"Seize life! Eat bread with gusto, drink wine with a robust heart.
Oh yes—God takes pleasure in your pleasure!"

—ECCLESIASTES 9:7 THE MESSAGE

Bread is a universal staple for all the people of the world. Even right now, somewhere in the world, friends and families are gathered together around a table breaking bread. It is an act of relationship and unity. Somewhere on this planet, loaves of bread are baking in a brick oven, clay pot, or wrapped in leaves over a fire pit.

" 'Give us today our daily bread.' "

—MATTHEW 6:11

Jesus said this is how we should pray to the Father. He also said that the Father knows what we need even before we ask. Before the sun rose this morning, before we ever got out of bed or prayed our first prayer of the day, He understood our needs and desires. He heard the deepest unspoken cries of our hearts. He knew we would need His daily bread. Some days He feeds us a sourdough variety and other days it's sweet zucchini bread with raisins. We never have to stand in line or worry about what kind of bread we will eat. He knows what we need to make it through the day. Our Father provides the perfect loaf of bread to nourish and strengthen us each day.

"Open wide your mouth and I will fill it."

—PSALM 81:10

We smell the wonderful, glorious aroma of the Bread of Life and we hunger for it! We must have it! When we taste it, we want more. This Bread fully sustains us. This Bread is life and health and peace. Jesus said, " 'I am the bread of life. He who comes to me will never go hungry' " (John 6:35).

In the Bible, we read about the little boy who sacrificed his lunch for others—giving all he had (John 6:1–15). Jesus multiplied the barley loaves and fish, and all who were gathered there benefited from this child's simple faith and generous heart. The people ate until they were full, and there were still baskets of bread and fish left over. There was enough food for today and more than enough for later. No one left the presence of Jesus hungry. There is no want or begging for bread in the kingdom of God. Instead, there is a wealth of daily provision. The supply is endless, everlasting, and eternal.

A FAITH THAT BREATHES

. . . *is rejuvenated by Christian fellowship.* Jesus often broke bread with those He encountered. The sharing of bread was more than the act of enjoying a meal. It was about relationship, communion, and being united as one. During the last meal He shared with His beloved disciples, Jesus gave thanks to the Father, broke the bread, and gave it to them, saying, " 'This is my body given for you; do this in remembrance of me' " (Luke 22:19).

. . . *knows that when we receive and remember the broken body of Jesus, we are healed and made whole.* We are forgiven and accepted in the family of God. We have the honor of coming to the table to share in the communion of breaking bread and to receive gratefully from the Father's generous hand.

. . . *consumes daily the Bread of Heaven, which is food for the soul.* Jesus is our Bread of Life, our abundant life. He is all we need. Daily. Receive, eat, and enjoy!

JILL PAQUETTE
Thoughts about Fish, Food, and the Bible

People are always asking me, "With a name like Paquette, what's your heritage?" I'm sure you're thinking that, too, so let me get this out of the way: I live in Canada, and I'm Matee. That means Native American/European. The European part could be Welsh or Irish or Scottish, but mine is French. I come from the Cree tribe and France. I guess it happened when the European settlers came to North America and took Native American wives. That's how the Matee people were formed. Literally translated, it also means half-breed.

I grew up going to church. Actually, my home life was great, and my family was a real inspiration to me. My mom is an awesome prayer warrior and my dad—wow, he has so much wisdom. He is also Mr. Outdoors Survival Guy, so we spent our free time hunting and fishing. Which brings me to what I want to talk about: cleaning fish.

It sounds weird, but as a kid, I really liked this task. It was always my job, and I really thought it was cool that I was entrusted with this responsibility. Looking back, I now see that it was really the fellowship that I enjoyed—not so much the stinky fish guts. And I enjoyed what happened after the fish was cleaned and cooked: breaking bread with the ones I loved. These are the memories that I hold onto.

Lately, I have spent a lot of time consuming spiritual bread: the Holy Bible. I've never read it all the way through. And I have come to realize that all I've ever done is have these answers that I use in Sunday school. You know, little Scriptures that I'll quote here and there. Yet I don't even know from the beginning to the finish what the Word of God says. I know it roughly, but I've never read it. What if Christianity is more than I think it is? I'm trying not to read any other books as I focus on the Bible.

And as I consume my daily Bread, I'm expecting God to do something amazing in me. I hope to have a deeper fellowship with Him—and a lot more fun than cleaning fish!

power of a praying saint

> And he who searches our hearts knows the mind of the
> Spirit, because the Spirit intercedes for the saints
> in accordance with God's will.
>
> —ROMANS 8:27

People described Julie's mother as quiet and gentle. She was not the kind of person who would demand to be heard or who would want to be the center of attention. She rarely raised her voice. She was humble and meek.

When she was blessed in Christ's presence, she didn't shout aloud or dance in the aisles, she just quietly bowed her head and cried.

Julie's mom would never think of praying loud or long in public, yet her family knew she went frequently to her prayer closet. Everyone could sense that she held an anointing from the heavenly realm in her heart. As a matter of fact, people in grocery stores or in waiting rooms—or anywhere the family would go—sought her out and asked her to remember them in prayer. Strangers asked prayers for healing and salvation; prayers for sons and daughters in the service or prodigals far away from God. People were drawn to her and to the Light she carried within.

Julie's father died unexpectedly at an early age, so her mother was left to raise Julie and her younger sister on her own. While the sister gave no one any trouble at all, Julie became a prodigal. Despite her mother's love and a solid Christian upbringing, Julie strayed from the faith. She attended church on Sundays, then lived a secret life outside of the sanctuary walls. Julie thought she had become an expert at fooling people with her dual roles. Yet her mother knew the truth all along. And her mother prayed without ceasing on her behalf.

"Lord, bring my prodigal child home," she'd cry out in her prayer closet. "Julie is hurting from the loss of her father. Have mercy on her, Lord! Put the desire to seek You above all things in her heart. Raise her up as a woman of God! Whatever it takes, Lord!"

• • •

We have not stopped praying for you and asking God to fill you with the knowledge of his will through all spiritual wisdom and understanding. And we pray this in order that you may live a life worthy of the Lord and may please him in every way.

—COLOSSIANS 1:9–10

Julie's mom often spoke the Word and believed—holding onto hope, the evidence of things not yet seen. Her faith had moved mountains. Still, her prodigal was far, far away.

Then the accident happened. A drunk driver hit the motorcycle on which Julie was riding, crushing her leg. She was rushed to emergency surgery, but the medical team was uncertain if her leg could be saved. Amputation was a very real probability. Julie's mother went to prayer as a warrior to battle.

> The Spirit helps us in our weakness. We do not know
> what we ought to pray for, but the Spirit himself
> intercedes for us with groans that words cannot express.
>
> —ROMANS 8:26

In and out of consciousness over the next few days, Julie remembered opening her eyes and seeing the sweet face of her mother, who was at her bedside, smoothing her hair and holding her hand. Even when Julie couldn't open her eyes, she could hear her mother's prayers being whispered on her behalf. Prayers of a saint were calling out to Jesus for Julie; the Word of God was spoken over her body and soul.

> And he who searches our hearts knows the mind of the Spirit,
> because the Spirit intercedes for the saints
> in accordance with God's will.
>
> —ROMANS 8:27

After several weeks of medical debate, the doctors decided not to amputate Julie's leg—because, miraculously, it had begun to heal! Her mother celebrated the answered prayer with tears. Then she left Julie's room, walked down to the hospital chapel, and worshiped Jesus.

> "Fear not, for I have redeemed you; I have summoned you by
> name; you are mine. When you pass through the waters,
> I will be with you; and when you pass through the rivers,
> they will not sweep over you. When you walk through the fire,
> you will not be burned; the flames will not set you ablaze."
>
> —ISAIAH 43:1–2

Although the prayers for Julie's healing were answered, it was still several more years before her mother witnessed the fruit of her labor in prayer. Eventually, the prayers of a praying saint brought Julie and her family back home—and into the heart of a spiritual awakening. God was in all of the details, and Julie was privileged to be a part of a spiritual move of the Holy Spirit—unlike any she had ever seen. Her life could not have been more blessed!

Were her mother's prayers answered? Absolutely! Did it happen overnight? Absolutely not.

Julie came home to the Father's house twenty-six years ago and has never left. Her desire to seek God in her life is stronger today than ever. She is devoted to being a woman of God. Her mother's prayers, spoken years ago, are still being answered. "God is faithful," Julie often tells others. "His promises are true."

> Now to him who is able to do immeasurably more than all we ask
> or imagine, according to his power that is at work within us. . .
>
> —EPHESIANS 3:20

Today, Julie herself is a mother—and she, too, has a prodigal child. Julie now knows of the magnitude and intensity of her mother's prayers over the years. And she, too, holds onto faith and hope that has no evidence of being seen. Not yet. However, she prays believing—not if but when!

Just like the father in the parable of the lost son, Julie stands waiting, watching in the distance, to see a first glimpse of her prodigal child on his way back to the Father's house.

> "While he was still a long way off, his father saw him and was filled with compassion for him. . . . So they began to celebrate."
>
> —LUKE 15:20, 24

A FAITH THAT BREATHES

. . . *understands the purpose of prayer.* Prayer is designed to get you on track with God's will not to adjust Him to your agenda. Here's how author Henry T. Blackaby explains it: "Prayer does not give you spiritual power. Prayer aligns your life with God so that He chooses to demonstrate His power through you. The purpose of prayer is not to convince God to change your circumstances, but to prepare you to be involved in God's activity."[1]

. . . *expects results during prayer.* Not only are we called to this divine activity (see Philippians 4:6 and 1 Timothy 2:1–3), we are guaranteed God's action in response to our prayers. As

2 Chronicles 20:14–17 points out, God wants us to lay our anxieties before Him in prayer. He will take our worries and walk with us. He will carry our problems and give us peace. But remember: God responds *on His terms, according to His will,* and *in His perfect timing.* So, if you've prayed and prayed without seeing the results you hoped for, maybe God has something else in mind. Refocus your prayers on what God wants to see happen in you.

JENNIFER KNAPP
How Prayer and Compassion Influenced My Life

During my college years, two Christian ladies befriended me—even though I was pretty hostile toward them.

Despite how I disagreed with their faith, they continued to establish a relationship with me and work on just becoming friends. As I got to know them and I got to see Christ in their lives in very real ways, I began to ask questions about what they believed. It became very intriguing to me.

Making an impression on somebody for the Lord requires an honest and legitimate relationship first. After we became friends, one girl, Paula, started giving Scripture to me explaining the death and resurrection of Christ a little bit. I was more open to what she had to say once I felt like she cared. My other friend, Amy, took a lot of persecution from me, too, but in the end, she ended up being the one who led me to Christ.

I began to ask questions because Amy really displayed her Christian faith in her day-to-day life. For instance, she would get up on Sunday mornings to go to church, and I thought that was extraordinarily bizarre for somebody who had a life in college. Her mom and dad weren't making her go, but she went anyway. I could see a difference in her. My Christian friends eventually got to see what God could do in my life when I got saved. They later became good leaders as far as discipleship is concerned, too.

I believe there's a place for street evangelism and missions work, where it's kind of in and out and very quick, just telling the basic truth of God. But there are also the times where you're a leader. It's not just wearing a T-shirt or putting up a poster, but it's the manner in which you conduct yourself—an excellence about your life. Whether it's at your school or at your job, it comes down to living out your Christian faith and not just talking about it. We can say what we want about Christ all day, but if other people don't see our faith portrayed in our lifestyle, it means very little.

body of believers

Consequently, you are no longer foreigners and aliens,
but fellow citizens with God's people and
members of God's household,
built on the foundation of the apostles and prophets,
with Christ Jesus himself as the chief cornerstone.
In him the whole building is joined together
and rises to become a holy temple in the Lord.
And in him you too are being built together
to become a dwelling in which God lives by his Spirit.

—EPHESIANS 2:19–22

"Christians are just a bunch of hypocrites!"

We hear slams like this repeatedly from unbelievers *and* believers alike. Yet, in all honesty, there is a bit of truth to this statement—at least at times in our lives, right?

Face it, those of us who label ourselves *Christian* can be some of the most prideful, self-righteous weirdos on the planet. We've made for ourselves a subculture with our own music, television stations, magazines, and newspapers. We manufacture our own line of jewelry with crosses, purity rings, and WWJD bracelets. We post bumper stickers on our cars claiming, "I'm not perfect, just forgiven," right next to a silver fish symbol.

There are "Christian only" housing communities. Christian business owners give discounts to those who say "I'm a Christian" or "I work at [fill-in-the-blank] ministry." We have our own buzzwords, such as *cell groups, megachurches, born again,* and *on fire.* The church we attend determines our status. Some of us even dress alike.

True story: When members of a liberal activist group wanted to see the inside of their radically conservative archenemy's headquarters, they arranged for a tour and arrived incognito, wearing outdated flowered dresses. Apparently they assumed all radically right-wing Christian women wore obnoxious floral fashions. (We can only assume they had a previous experience upon which to base that assumption.)

But hey, in this day and age, we're all caught up in the perks and quirks of subcultural Christianity. Besides, saving a few bucks in car repairs with the Christian discount isn't so bad—right?

Actually, maybe it's time to readjust our thinking.

Do you find yourself following the *Christian* crowd? Is your faith based on the latest self-help book written by a respected Christian author? If someone asked you why you believe in Jesus Christ and the Bible, can you give an answer *without* using *Christianese?*

What does it mean to truly be a member of the body of Christ?

• • •

We're talking about real faith and real Christianity here.

To find out what this faith is all about, we must look to the source, to the foundation of our faith, the very cornerstone: Jesus Christ. What did He say about His body, the Church? Fortunately, John's gospel outlines in detail Jesus' prayer in the garden of Gethsemane. Without John's insight, we would still be speculating on what was going through Jesus' mind during those early morning hours before He was crucified. In this particular prayer, found in John 17, our Lord prayed for Himself, for His disciples, and for all believers—which includes you and me. He thought of us that night. What exactly did He petition His Father for on our behalf?

" 'My prayer is not for them alone. I pray also for those who will believe in me through their message, that all of them may be one, Father, just as you are in me and I am in you' " (John 17:20–21). His desire was for the body of believers to be united with each other and with Him. Okay, so maybe it isn't necessarily *wrong* for us Christians to love the time we have together. Even complete strangers can be instantly bonded with one another through a common commitment to Christ.

Fellowship with the body of Christ is a good thing. It's necessary for the good health of a believer.

Recently, while I (Johanna) was on a train in Paris, a couple took the two seats next to mine. They asked me, in English, if the seats were taken. I smiled at hearing my native tongue spoken and quickly moved my bags. When they were seated, I asked, "Where are you from?" It turned out they were both pastors from Maryland.

The wife had accepted a year-long position as liaison for their denomination's churches around the globe. The husband was a hospital chaplain. By the end of our conversation, I was greatly encouraged, and we blessed each other as we parted.

I'm sure you have your own stories about meeting fellow brothers and sisters in Christ along life's road, sensing that eternal bond, and coming away with uplifted spirits. It's something I cherish about being a part of the body of Christ.

" 'May they be brought to complete unity to let the world know that you sent me and have loved them even as you have loved me' " (John 17:23). How convicting! Does the world around me know that God sent His Son, Jesus? Does my life indicate that Jesus loves them as much as God loves Jesus?

Again and again, Jesus emphasized unity in the body. If there were disunity, the world would have a hard time believing in Christ as Savior. If we do not love each other, we cannot show Christlike love to others. This love must be flowing inside the body and flowing to all those we encounter.

The body of believers is not defined by a church building. It spans the entire globe. The body works together, not just to host potlucks after Sunday morning service but to feed the physically and spiritually hungry. The body must be united in the cause of Jesus Christ. It must tell the world that God loves them so much that He put His Son on the sacrificial altar so that we can spend eternity with Him.

Here's something you can do in your next quiet time with our Lord: Pick out your favorite instrumental song and pop it into your CD player. Read Jesus' prayer in John 17 as the music plays in the background. Listen to His words come alive with passion, and thank Him for praying for you that early morning in Gethsemane.

A FAITH THAT BREATHES

. . .*sees the body of Christ as one functioning unit.*
There will always be disagreements in the church. It is to be expected with imperfect humans. However, God desires unity in purpose. We must strive toward the goal of a unified body.

. . .*encourages other members in their purpose.*
Some communities of believers worship God by dancing and waving flags. Others worship God by reverent singing of hymns passed down from believers long past. I could write an entire twelve-volume set of differences in the body of believers, but I won't. I'd rather encourage my brothers and sisters in their own gifts and talents and find ways to work together to reflect the character of Christ to a lost world.

JOY WILLIAMS
Let's Be Real with Each Other

When I was in high school, I liked to be the girl who appeared to have everything together. It seemed safer to pretend than to be vulnerable. Since then, however, God has been teaching me to have the faith to believe that the way He made me is okay. I'm getting better at not feeling so insecure.

I've asked God to break me. It seems like an odd request, and it's been a painful one. And yet, I'm finding that God has been meeting me every place I've been. My faith has been built up so much.

Through it all, know what I've discovered? We need other Christians. It's okay to lean on someone when we feel weak. To truly become who God wants us to be, we need a body of believers.

Sometimes I can't help asking myself, "Who am I? Why am I here? Who even cares about me?" But I have a solid Christian sister, a mentor, who keeps me connected with God. She'll look me in the eyes and say, "Joy, remember who you are in Christ. Remember that when God sees you, He smiles. When God thinks of you, He doesn't think of everything that's wrong. He thinks of everything that's right, because you're His princess."

a woman
of influence

the Proverbs 31 woman

Charm is deceptive, and beauty is fleeting;

but a woman who fears the LORD is to be praised.

Give her the reward she has earned,

and let her works bring her praise at the city gate.

—PROVERBS 31:30–31

It was Christmas Eve—a joyful time, a family time. So why did I (Michael) feel so depressed? For one thing, my mom and I were alone.

I was seventeen, and my five older siblings (three brothers and two sisters) were grown up and out of the house—and unable to come home for the holidays. As for my father, he had deserted my family when I was a young boy.

The truth is, Dad was an alcoholic—and Mom would never allow alcohol in our house. So, when I was still young enough to need training wheels on my bike, Mom was forced to take a tough love approach. She told my dad, "Get help, and learn to be a proper husband and a father, or follow your addiction—and lose your family. You can't have both."

My father chose his addiction. It was a decision that broke our hearts and cracked the foundation of my family. Yet, in the years that followed, my mother was determined to mend some of the fractures and hold our family together. I'm happy to say she succeeded. (To this day, my brothers, sisters, and I share a deep bond that was nurtured by our mother.)

But on this particular Christmas, I didn't feel very festive. I missed the chaotic Grand Central Station atmosphere that usually filled our house.

"Yep, this is going to be a sorry holiday," I mumbled to myself as I slouched down in a recliner and stared glumly at our Christmas tree.

Does this thing actually have branches? I wondered. Our tree was covered with so many ornaments and candy canes and strands of popcorn, it was nearly impossible to see anything that was remotely sprucelike.

I squinted, noticing a brightly colored decoration that I had made years earlier and a few that had been created by my sisters. *Mom has saved them all,* I thought to myself. *This tree is like a timeline of our lives.*

As I followed the "timeline," memories began to flood my mind. Mostly good ones.

My eyes focused on an oddly shaped antique bulb that had been passed down from my grandmother. I couldn't help thinking about all the family traditions my mom had established. She was so proud of our heritage. (My relatives could be traced back to England, Scotland, and Sweden.)

I spotted a furry, hand-stitched reindeer my mom had made—which triggered images of the long hours she worked cooking, cleaning, and doing everything possible to keep a roof over our heads.

Suddenly, my thoughts were interrupted by the sweet smell of chocolate—then a warm smile.

"Let's open a gift," my mom said, handing me a cup of cocoa. "We always open one present on Christmas Eve—and this year shouldn't be any different." Before I had a chance to utter a word, she plopped a big package on my lap.

"No, Mom, let's just forget about it," I protested. "Everything's all wrong this year."

Mom lifted an eyebrow. "I'd say things are pretty right," she replied.

I shook my head and groaned. My mom continued talking.

"Look around you," she said. "Look at where you live, and consider the food you get to eat. Some people in the world don't have any of these things. And think about the people who love you—like your brothers and sisters. They may not be here physically. . .but we're still a family. A strong family."

Secretly, I was tracking with everything my mom had to say, but my teenage pride wouldn't allow me to admit it. Instead, I glanced at the package on my lap and gently began tugging at the ribbon. When the last piece of wrapping paper fell to the floor, the gift was revealed.

I looked up and gasped. "Mom—you can't afford this!"

"I'm the gift-giver here. . .so I'll decide what I can and can't afford."

My mom had practically emptied her savings account on a present that I had talked endlessly about for years, yet had always thought was out of reach. She had bought me a 35mm camera, complete with a variety of lenses.

"Every young journalist should learn to use a camera, right?" Mom asked.

I sat speechless, feeling as if I was holding more than just a camera—but some sort of link to my future. "This is amazing!" I said as I fiddled with the gadgets.

"There's a carrying bag in the box, too," Mom said. "I figure you can take this to college with you next year."

A grin stretched across my face. "Mom, you're pretty amazing. You sacrifice so much for us. What would we do without you? Who would we be?"

Suddenly, Christmas didn't seem so empty. And from that moment on, I began to see my mom differently. For the first time during my teen years, I began to respect her for the incredible woman God had created her to be. And from that moment on, my world began to make a lot more sense.

• • •

That night, I unwrapped the greatest gift a teen could ever receive. I don't mean an expensive camera, of course. I'm talking about the gift of *hope*. Despite the hardships in our lives, my mom did everything possible to shape her children into men and women who were ready to face the world with confidence. She planted seeds of faith in our lives and sparked in us a vision for the future.

When I think of my mother—and the profound influence she has had on so many people, Proverbs 31 comes to mind. Although this passage refers specifically to "a wife of noble character," the verses highlight some qualities and spiritual principles that all women can apply. But keep in mind, these verses refer to the ideal. They are goals for which to strive.

The Proverbs 31 woman. . .

. . .is trustworthy (v. 10): Reliable. Can be counted on. Consistent. Secure. Realistic.

. . .is virtuous (v. 11): Morally upright. Learns from past mistakes and keeps her principles.

. . .is industrious (vv. 13–14, 28): Hardworking. Diligent. Active, busy, persistent. She hangs in there with tough tasks when her body and mind tell her to quit.

. . .is generous (v. 15): Unselfish. Considerate. Kindhearted. Ungrudging. Always willing to give or share.

. . .is wise (vv. 16, 27): Perceptive. Intuitive. Thoughtful. Shrewd. Aims for practical, God-honoring goals.

. . .is strong (v. 17): Stable, sure of herself. She has the ability to juggle many different tasks under pressure.

. . .is compassionate (v. 19): Sympathetic, responsive, and warm. Willing to offer constructive help.

. . .is dignified (v. 28): Stands tall with grace. Poised.

. . .is spiritual (v. 30): Fears God and reveres her relationship with Him above everything else.

A FAITH THAT BREATHES

. . .*strives to be a "woman of noble character."* With God's help, you can become the woman God desires you to be. Use Proverbs 31 as a standard to reach for, knowing that you don't have to fulfill every detail in every verse.

. . .*puts God above everything in life.* Regardless of your gifts and goals, make sure that Proverbs 31:30 is true for you: "A woman who fears the LORD is to be praised."

KIM HILL
Charm Is Deceitful

If I had to choose one message to share with women today, it would be this: "You are precious to God and very important to Him. Regardless of how you look on the outside, He loves you and will never let you down. He is your friend and He is faithful. He would die on the cross for you—even if you were the only person on earth."

I'm saddened by how much time women spend worrying about what's on the outside, while neglecting the inside—their character. Several years ago, I recorded a song called "Charm Is Deceitful"—which is based on Proverbs 31:30.

> *Charm is deceitful*
> *Beauty is vain*
> *But a woman who fears the Lord shall be praised. . .*
> *In a world where we see with our eyes*
> *I pray for eyes that see the heart. . .*

Looking good is important, but it's not good to get so caught up in our looks. It's tough to balance concern for our appearance with concern for who we are on the inside—the part of us that lasts forever. I often ask myself, *Do I spend as much time with the Lord, developing my spirit, as I do exercising?*

Through the years, the Lord has given me compassion for other people. He's helped me to focus on their character—not just their clothes and hair and things on the surface.

Learning to look at myself and others through God's eyes has been a difficult challenge for me. (It's just human nature to look at the "package," isn't it?) Yet I've sought to follow the example of my two greatest role models: my mom and dad. I've always been really close to my parents. I never went through any big rebellion as a teen. They were my loudest testimony of all the Lord could be in my life.

In high school, my mom really nurtured my spiritual growth. She'd come into my room in the mornings and say, "Kim, get up. Read your Bible." And I would try, but it was a real struggle. I had a hard time being consistent and faithful. I'd get frustrated and think, *Why is this so hard? Why can't I do this?*

Even though I became a Christian when I was nine, I didn't really grasp the concept of entire commitment until college. I eventually asked God to take my whole life and to have all of me. At that point, I had a real desire to read the Word and spend time with Him. In fact, spending the start of each day with the Lord is now the most important thing I do. When I miss a day with Him, I really notice a difference.

I've also learned to step back, take a break from my daily routine, and ask myself a few hard-core questions: *What are my priorities? What am I really living for—God or things?*

I'm doing my best to be faithful to the Lord. The one thing I want to urge young women to do is spend time with Jesus now and walk with Him today—don't wait until tomorrow. Give Him your youthful years. He'll use what you have and will honor the desires of your heart. I guarantee it!

roles and current culture

> Let the peace of Christ rule in your hearts,
> since as members of one body you were called to peace.
> And be thankful. Let the word of Christ dwell in you richly
> as you teach and admonish one another with all wisdom,
> and as you sing psalms, hymns and spiritual songs
> with gratitude in your hearts to God.
> And whatever you do, whether in word or deed,
> do it all in the name of the Lord Jesus,
> giving thanks to God the Father through him.
>
> —COLOSSIANS 3:15–17

The suspense was agonizing.

Special Agent Janell Salveson gripped her .38 revolver, aimed it at the front door of the house, and froze.

Two other agents fanned out on each side of her, while another pair sneaked to the back of the house. A sixth agent hugged a wall and inched his way to the porch.

The FBI had learned that this address was the hideout of a dangerous fugitive. Now they were moving in for the arrest.

"Come out with your hands up," yelled an agent.

"The place is completely surrounded!"

Silence. Then, faint movement somewhere inside.

"This is the FBI. Give it up—*now*!"

Again, silence.

Janell took a deep breath and swallowed. She was prepared for the worst.

Suddenly, the lead agent reared back his leg and thrust it against the door with massive force.

His foot connected with the weathered wood— then kept going. He punched a hole through the bottom half of the rickety door, then stood helpless. He was stuck.

What would happen next? Would bullets begin to fly? Would the FBI get their man—without losing one of their own?

Seconds later, the door burst open and a confused mother cradling a baby in her arms stuck out her head. She looked at the hole in her door and gasped.

The FBI received a bad tip; their fugitive was nowhere in sight.

Janell put away her gun and smiled. *Thank You, Lord. The only casualty was a rickety old door—and maybe a few nerves.*

• • •

"It was like a scene from a TV comedy," Janell laughs, looking back. "But it doesn't always turn out that way. You have to be prepared for anything in this business."

Janell has served as a special agent for the FBI for many years. During her long career, she has fingerprinted plenty of fugitives, cracked down on countless kidnappers, investigated a bunch of bank robberies, and wiped out a whirlwind of white-collar crime, such as bank fraud. She even spent some time chasing spies.

"It's officially called 'foreign counterintelligence,' " Janell says. "It was my job to stop the 'intelligence' attempts of foreign countries that are hostile to the United States. In other words, I monitored the activities of spies, reported their activities, and stopped them from gaining technology or selling important secrets to other countries."

Sounds like there's never a dull moment for this agent. Yet what's it like working in a field that's dominated by men? "Actually, times they are a-changin'," Janell says. "While females are definitely outnumbered in my line of work, the bureau is looking for a few good *women* to wear their badge.

"But in today's culture, where male/female roles are also changing, the question I get asked most is, 'Doesn't your faith in God collide with your job?' My answer: It pulls me through tough situations and makes me a better agent. My faith is as necessary to me as breathing; I wouldn't want to do any job without it. It's like my skin; it's part of me. And that's how it should be—no matter what badge you wear and regardless of whether you're male or female."

Some Christians would criticize women like Janell, claiming that she's not fulfilling a traditional role. Others would applaud her. How do you feel about this issue? And what does the Bible say?

Actually, God's Word does not suggest that women should sit passively at home, waiting to serve their men. To the contrary, Scripture indicates that women should be productive.

In the popular passage on the characteristics of a noble or virtuous woman, Proverbs 31 (flip back to yesterday's lesson), we find a woman engaged in real estate transactions and business endeavors that turn a profit. She demonstrates managerial skills, as well as benevolence to the poor, caring for the family, and serving the Lord. It is important to note that her husband is considered blessed by his peers because he has such an industrious wife. Obviously, neither one of them was threatened by the success of the other. This is as good a model for today as it was for yesterday.

So whether you're chasing spies or chasing toddlers, take Janell's advice: Make your faith as "necessary as breathing." Don't take on any role without God as the foundation.

A FAITH THAT BREATHES

. . .*strives to never lose its identity.* It's okay to express yourself through the clothes you wear or to excel at a talent or ability. But if you try to base your total identity on those things, you'll end up losing your identity. What's more, you'll end up bitterly disappointed.

. . .*lets God be God.* Ask Him to tear down idols

in your life—a relationship, a job, a posses-
sion. . .anything that you value more than
Him. Keep in mind that, in the world's eyes,
your identity is wrapped up in roles and
appearances—what you do, how smart or ath-
letic you are, and how you look. But in God's
eyes, what matters is who you are—His child.

. . .*is grounded in God.* Our Lord wants the very
best for you. His plans for you are even better
than your wildest dreams. Jesus doesn't look at
you and say, "This is who you are—and who
you'll always be." Instead, He says, "Just imagine who you can become!"

SARA GROVES
We Each Juggle Multiple Roles

Identifying my many roles isn't always easy: I'm a wife, a mother, a songwriter, and a storyteller. And some describe me as a preacher whose pulpit is a piano bench. Each of these titles describes me. Yet the whole music thing isn't exactly something that I chose—but I do take this role very seriously. I'm now convinced that I've been called to it.

When I think about my music career, my grandfather comes to mind. While he could build things and worked with his hands, I work with words. I feel that one of my strengths is to give people tools. Music can be a tool to come to grips with your relationship with God and your relationships with others.

Not everyone is good with words or emotions, and I feel as if that's what I do—I put words to people's emotions so they can work through them and move on to the next level with God.

As a CCM artist, I feel that I'm part of something much bigger than myself. It's God's math. The Lord multiplies everything so that people I've never met before, in places I've never traveled, are being affected. Not that if I quit the ministry the world would fall apart. But I do know that if I don't play my part, people miss out.

The important thing for women to believe is that we all have a part—and not to let anyone tell us that we cannot play our part.

The world throws away people who aren't useful. God says everyone who has breath is useful in His kingdom. We simply have to believe this and know that it's true. If anyone doesn't play his or her part in the kingdom, we all miss out.

a girl of grace

"But while he was still a long way off, his father saw him
and was filled with compassion for him; he ran to his son,
threw his arms around him and kissed him. . . . 'Quick!
Bring the best robe and put it on him. Put a ring on his
finger and sandals on his feet. Bring the fattened calf and
kill it. Let's have a feast and celebrate. For this son of mine
was dead and is alive again; he was lost and is found.' "

—LUKE 15:20, 22–24

Once upon a time, an actress in Hollywood, already
blessed with great beauty and poise, was courted by and
then married a wealthy prince who had fallen deeply
in love with her.

True story. Her name and title became Princess
Grace. What a wonderful name to have. I (Vanessa) can't
imagine being known throughout the world as "Princess
Grace." She was one of those select few whose name
reflected exactly what you saw in her. She did have wonderful grace. Her manner was gentle and certain, and the
camera never seemed to catch her unaware, without her
beatific smile and her hand outstretched to be kissed
by royalty. I can't imagine what her life must have been
like, so privileged and so accepted by the world.

There are others whose names come to mind when I hear the word *grace*. For example, Fred Astaire and Ginger Rogers. They danced so beautifully together. Have you seen their movie, *Carefree*? There is a particular dance scene that plays out like a dream. The duo glides across the screen with such agility and poise—every movement filled with grace. Grace is a beautiful thing.

• • •

I have grace. In fact, it has been poured into my life so greatly that I can never spend an entire day without being grateful for it. Of course, it's not the same kind of grace that a princess or a pair of dancers might have. On the contrary, I have very little of that kind of grace.

When I was a teenager, I was always clumsy. One day, I asked my mother why. She replied (and it is a joke between us to this day) that it was just a phase and I would grow out of it. I am wondering now, twenty-some years later, exactly when I will be growing out of it.

My kind of grace comes in a very different form. It comes from God. It was bought with a great price, and it is limitless. In fact, the grace I have will last long after I'm past my dancing days. It will last even into eternity.

It isn't just an asset that causes people to like me, although I am sure it does make me easier to live with. Yet it's much more essential than that. This kind of grace is like breath to a stifled soul. It comes in like a gush of water when I am in my driest seasons. It offers freedom from cares and worries too big for me to handle. I just call out to God and He sends it. With God, every prayer is heard, and every sin is forgiven.

The grace I'm referring to is the gift from God of sins forgiven and the assurance of eternal fellowship with Him.

In truth, we don't deserve this gift. (This is why it's called *grace.)* It is freely given—and absolutely undeserved.

We can earn lots of things in life, but we have no way of earning grace from God. Grace is almost beyond our cognitive grasp. To be able to imagine a concept so completely different than anything this life will ever teach us requires much meditation and contemplation. Yet if we stop for just a few minutes to try to understand grace, we find our mind opening up to the nature of God. We begin to see His heart for us. We begin to sense His boundless love for His creation.

A FAITH THAT BREATHES

. . .understands that God's grace is completely selfless.
We can often do things that seem selfless, but if we chase our motives to the very end, we find they are always for reasons that pertain to us first and others second. But God's heart toward us is pure. Even His insistence that we honor His name stems from the fact that His name is our only hope. There simply is no other name given to us by which we can be saved. So He protects it because we need it.

. . .knows that when we fail and fumble in life, God's grace is there waiting for us. When we face trials that are too big for us to handle, we can cry out to God, and He offers His grace. God's Holy Spirit comes to us and strengthens us, guides us, lifts us up, shows us a way out. The Lord gives us courage, teaches us through love and gentle correction, and protects us from things we don't even realize we need protection from. He reminds us of the price that Jesus already paid.

. . .rejoices in the good news that grace is ours for the asking. That's right—just for the asking! If we are good, God will pour out His grace on us. If we are bad, God will pour out His grace on us. It's hard to comprehend, but it's the truth. God's grace is powerful, abundant, eternal— and absolutely free. God is faithful. It pleases Him to give us His grace. All you have to do is ask for it.

POINT OF GRACE
God, Guys. . .and Grace

This multiple Dove Award–winning, gold- and platinum-selling vocal group has been sharing their faith through music for more than a decade. Their highly successful Girls of Grace conferences have inspired young ladies to lead pure, godly lives. Their best-selling book and CD by the same title is continuing to change lives. In the paragraphs that follow, Point of Grace shares their thoughts on God, guys. . .and grace.

Heather, on "A Guide for Girls"

One of the very first songs I ever learned was "The B-I-B-L-E." Remember that song? "The B-I-B-L-E, yes, that's the book for me. I stand alone on the Word of God, the B-I-B-L-E." I love that song. As a matter of fact, I've heard Denise's son Spence sing it a few times, and I must say that every time I hear it, it brings back memories of going to vacation Bible school and Sunday school.

You know, it's not easy to live life the way God wants us to. How can you stand up against the temptations and difficulties? How can you be an obedient daughter and kind sister? How can you behave purely and righteously? The writer of Psalm 119 asks these questions and gives you the answer: "How can a young person stay pure? By obeying your word and following its rules" (verse 9 NLT). You can't very well obey God's Word and follow its rules if you don't know what it says. Spending time in His Word is a key ingredient to keeping yourself pure.[2]

Denise, on "God with Us"

A few years back, my husband experienced some hip troubles. When he had it checked out, doctors found a tumor in his thighbone. While we were waiting for his test results, we went into the studio to record a song titled "Blue Skies." I had the solo and had to sing it during the waiting time, not knowing whether his tumor was malignant. The message of the song is this: In times of trouble, God sees us through. As the words went through my head, it was almost supernatural. God was with me: "No matter what the outcome, I am here with you."

Through five days of waiting for the test results, I thought about those lyrics a lot. It turned out the tumor was benign, and my husband was fine. The truth behind those lyrics really sustained us. God was right there with us, helping us through the fear—comforting our hearts.

Terry, on "The Ideal Guy"

Don't get married or date because it's the thing to do—because everyone you know is getting married or dating. Hearing so much about divorces has made me so glad that I have my husband, Chris, in my life. He's my perfect match. I can't imagine being with anybody else.

Marriage is such a wonderful thing that you really need to have it be with the right guy. If that means you're forty before you get married, then you wait for that guy and don't compromise yourself in any way.

Shelley, on "Grace at Home"

Life is not about getting our way but about pleasing God and doing things His way, and it's about being mature enough to handle it when we don't get to do exactly what we please.

Our parents deserve our respect and obedience simply because they are our parents. As a young woman trying to follow Christ and imitate Him, honoring and obeying your mom and dad are some of the most important fundamental things you can do to show your love for Him.[3]

(To read more from Point of Grace, pick up their book *Girls of Grace*, published by Howard Publishing.)

leading the way

> "Whoever wants to become great among you must
> be your servant, and whoever wants to be first
> must be your slave—just as the Son of Man
> did not come to be served, but to serve."
>
> —MATTHEW 20:26–28

Imagine yourself blasting into outer space. As the orbiter rockets at four to five times the speed of sound, your body is pressed back into your seat. (You actually now weigh twice your normal weight—*ugh!*)

Now imagine that thundering plume of fire and smoke is taking you to an orbiting space station or maybe even to Mars. Best of all, you're a bright young woman *and* an astronaut, excelling in a field once dominated by men. Even better, you're a woman of faith, a servant whom God is using to fulfill His eternal plans.

If this is your desire, it can happen—just ask shuttle astronaut Shannon Lucid. She holds down the fort in Houston, where she's a wife and mother of two daughters and one son. She's also part of NASA's space shuttle team as a mission specialist. For more than two decades, she has served among those with "the right stuff."

"It's truly a dream come true for me," she says. "I was hired by NASA in 1978 and went on my first mission aboard *Discovery*. Ever since I can remember, I wanted to be an astronaut.

"As a young woman, I was a real oddball," Shannon continues. "When I went to high school and college, everyone expected girls to do one thing: Grow up and be housewives. This is a noble pursuit, and I ended up becoming one, too—at least part-time. But I knew God had other plans for me, as well. I knew it involved space exploration."

With the direction of her Lord and the support of her husband and family, she set off into the great unknown—literally. (To date, she has logged more than eight hundred hours in space.)

"But if God isn't behind it," she points out, "I wouldn't be, either." This, she says, should be a Christian's most important desire: becoming the leader He desires—the one who sets the standard.

Does this describe you?

Regardless of your profession, regardless of your gifts and talents, what do you suppose are the characteristics you possess that are most valued by Him? What do you think He is trying to nurture in you?

Most important of all, what will it take for you to be a woman who is set apart by God—a woman who leads the way?

• • •

As popular author Henry T. Blackaby points out, "He will take whatever time is necessary to grow your character to match His assignment for you. . . . Character-building can be long and painful. It took twenty-five years before God entrusted Abraham with his first son and set in motion the establishment of the nation of Israel. Yet God was true to His Word."[4]

A woman who leads the way possesses five distinct character qualities. She

- loves God with all her heart, mind, and soul.

- lays down her life for others.

- humbles herself, taking on the very nature of a servant.

- nurtures love, joy, peace, patience, kindness, goodness, faithfulness, gentleness, self-control.

- walks with honor, integrity, holiness, and purity.

Consider the observations of A.W. Tozer: "If the church is to prosper spiritually, she must have spiritual leadership, not leadership by majority vote. It is highly significant that when the apostle Paul found it necessary to ask for obedience among the young churches, he never appealed to them on the grounds that he had been duly elected to office. He asserted his authority as an apostle appointed by the Head of the church. He held his position by right of sheer spiritual ascendancy, the only earthly right that should be honored among the children of the new creation."[5]

. . .*doesn't focus on the world.* Make an effort to feel secure in who God made you to be. Following the crowd just to fit in is one of Satan's traps. Vow to break the cycle now!

. . .*allows the Holy Spirit and the truth of the Bible to saturate your heart, mind, and soul.* This is an essential key to building leadership. Here's how author David Jeremiah explains it: "God will not prostitute His power to give us desires that will in the end be destructive to our walk with Him. But if we are consumed with a passion to find God's will through His Word and His Holy Spirit, we can always be in the place where God can shower down His power upon us."[6]

. . .*asks God to mold you.* Pray this: "Lord, shape my character as You prepare me to fulfill Your purpose." Ask Jesus to grow you into a young woman who is far stronger, far more obedient than you presently are. Ask Him to show you how to be faithful with the small assignments—always preparing you to handle even bigger tasks.

CRISTI JOHNSON (ALATHEA)

Leading the Way with Truth

The first time we formally played—"formally" meaning "in front of people"—we were the opener for a concert at Milligan College. We were told we needed a name for the group to put on the posters that would promote the show. My bandmate Carrie asked her dad, who knows Greek, to tell her some Greek words. When he said, "Alathea," she responded, "That's pretty—what does it mean?" He said, "Truth." Carrie scribbled it down on all the posters, and that was our beginning.

Not long afterward, Cristi and her band mates—Carrie Theobald and Mandee Radford—released their first album with Rocketown Records, titled *What Light Is All About.* Alathea's self-described "Popalacian" sound is acoustic in nature, with a mix of eclectic influences that reflect their Appalachian roots and diverse musical tastes. In the paragraphs that follow, Cristi speaks for the band, sharing her insights on truth, peace, God—and finding faith in a faithless world.

Insights on "Splinters"
I think that most of us who grew up in church have no trouble seeing the splinters in everyone else's eyes, but we don't know what to do with the log in our own eye. Sometimes, we don't even know how it got there. We recorded a song called "Runaway Heart." It's not about forsaking God in a single, big mistake but about the series of small decisions that lead

us away from the heart of God. Things like choosing not to love a brother. Compassion comes when we realize that our wandering hearts are all the same—and that we all need to find our way home.

Insights on "Finding God in the Quiet Places"

Carrie, Mandee, and I share a cabin that is situated four miles from the Appalachian Trail, which is a footpath that extends from Georgia to Maine and crosses our road at Iron Mountain Gap. When we're home, we spend lots of time on a small section of it. We run, hike, and walk the dog. Some people hike the entire trail in a few months. That feat seems impossible, but then, life does, too.

Indian Creek runs in front of our cabin—we wrote a song about that, as well. We go fishing there often, though we never seem to catch anything. But somehow, in that still, quiet place, God catches us—and He opens our eyes to see Him all around us.

Insights on "What the Lord Requires"

The prophet Micah asks, "With what shall I come before the Lord. . .with burnt offerings? . . .with thousands of rams? Shall I offer my firstborn. . .the fruit of my body?"(Micah 6:6–7). Don't try to complicate your faith with all kinds of trendy works. "What does the Lord require of you? To act justly and to love mercy and to walk humbly with your God" (v. 8).

reflecting His love

"Then the King will say to those on his right,

'Come, you who are blessed by my Father;

take your inheritance, the kingdom prepared for you

since the creation of the world.

For I was hungry and you gave me something to eat,

I was thirsty and you gave me something to drink,

I was a stranger and you invited me in,

I needed clothes and you clothed me,

I was sick and you looked after me,

I was in prison and you came to visit me.' "

—MATTHEW 25:34–36

Who do you think of when you read the words "reflecting His love"? Images of Mother Teresa and Jim Elliot flash through my mind. The ubiquitous cliché—"What Would Jesus Do?"—feels like the right question to ask when confronted with a situation that calls for His love.

Yet you may say to yourself, *I could never willingly preach the gospel to a cannibalistic tribe. I hope God never asks me to live in poverty.*

Some will never know the supernatural boldness given by God to accomplish the difficult tasks He asks of us. Others already have experienced His overflowing love and grace spilling over to everyone around. However, you may be wondering whether you would be able to reflect His love under extreme circumstances.

I (Johanna) want to introduce you to someone who happens to be my best friend. We have been friends for a long time, but we didn't start to get close until my sophomore year in high school. That was the year I decided to talk to him more often than just a friendly greeting or an occasional "thank you" when he opened a door for me or helped in one way or another. That was the year I decided to get to know him better. We began to talk briefly a few times a week. He had written me letters, which I would read at night, falling asleep to his caring words. Another friend of mine noticed something different about me. She said that I seemed to "shine" and smile a whole lot more lately.

Our new level of friendship had an effect on me. Like my circle of friends, for example. I was trying to be accepted by the "popular" kids at school. My friend had been rejected several times by others, and I knew the pain that had caused him. He told me that outward appearance and material things did not matter, but it was what was on the inside of a person that counted. So I tried to see the heart of people, no matter what others labeled them, and I actually found some lifetime friendships.

My friend is the best listener and gives the best advice. Through the years, I have cried to him about a broken relationship or a job that didn't work out, and he has always been ready to listen. Every time, I come away with a peace, knowing that God is still taking care of me. He always reminds me how faithful God is to accomplish the plans He has for me. He says he prays for me, especially when I don't know how to pray. I can always trust him at his word.

As time goes by, our relationship grows deeper. He knows how to make me smile. He'll point out a beautiful flower on one of our walks or tell me to look outside at the beautiful sunset over the mountains. He loves to surprise me with a note of encouragement or gift just when I need it. I now talk to him about *everything:* the guy I'm interested in, my day at work, what's happening around the world, and the deepest desires of my heart. He's also great to go shopping with because he'll tell me what to get for Christmas and birthday presents. I feel free to confess to him all my sins because I know he will accept me and help me through the darkness. When we are reading the Bible together, the words from a familiar passage suddenly come alive. When my friends and I go to his house, we have incredible times singing, laughing, and learning.

It is because of him that my other friendships are so close. It is because of his encouragement to me that I can encourage other people. His generosity toward me makes me want to be generous to others. His compassion, kindness, love, and faithfulness to everyone spur me on to be the same. I want to be just like him.

My best friend, as you may have guessed, is the Lord Jesus Christ. My faith in Him becomes more real the more I make Him a part of my life. It might sound silly to ask Him what clothes to wear the next day or what Christmas present I should buy for the person whose name I drew from the hat. But it is in these small things that I can learn to practice my faith and recognize His voice. If I only wait for the major decisions in life, like what job to accept or who to marry, the decision will be fraught with anxiety, making it that much more difficult. I want to reflect His love in every decision and action. Therefore, I invite Him into every circumstance, big or small.

We learn what real faith is by spending as much time with Him as possible—taking Him along when we are running errands, asking Him for wisdom in a new relationship, learning what His voice sounds like when He speaks to us. In Philippians 4:6, Paul urges his readers to "not be anxious about anything, but in everything, by prayer and petition, with thanksgiving, present your requests to God." I take that very literally. I want to come to a point where I am not anxious about the outcomes of my decisions because I have assurance that I have discussed the situation with my Lord and He has led me in the direction He wills. Therefore, I pray and tell the Lord every request and question I have. He'll answer me one way or another—possibly not the way I would have liked, but His way is always best.

Finally, spending more time facing His mirror (His Word) will inevitably cast a sharper image of His character back on us. His Word reveals the blemishes that only His medicine can heal. Let His Word make you beautiful, instead of using your own means to cover up your sin. In other words, let Him make you a reflection of His wonderful love shining out to everyone in your world. Put his love into action instead of just hearing about it at church (see James 1:22–25).

A FAITH THAT BREATHES

. . . *communicates to God about everything.* I find God's command to communicate with Him about everything all over in His Word. Throughout time, humanity has been given opportunities to communicate to the God of the universe. Before Jesus came to earth, humanity had to rely on priests and prophets to communicate to God. Then Jesus bridged the gap between humanity and God so now we talk and listen to Him wherever we go and whatever we do. In fact, it is a command to always pray. (For starters, check out 1 Thessalonians 5:17–18; Philippians 4:6; Romans 12:12; Ephesians 6:18.)

. . . *learns to obey the Lord.* When you are walking in obedience to Him, you are automatically a reflection of God's love. Jonah is famous for not immediately obeying God's command to share God's love with the city of Nineveh. God's powerful love moved the people away from evil once Jonah obeyed (Jonah 3:1–10).

. . .will inevitably reflect God's love to others. Remember, it is not your own reflection of love that people will see; it is God's love in you. Real faith demonstrates real love to the world. Love is an action not an emotional high. To get a general sense of what God's love looks like in everyday life, meditate on 1 Corinthians 13 and 1 John.

TRICIA BROCK
(SUPERCHIC[K])
The Face of Friendship

When I was in high school, I remember making a decision to lay down my life for Christ and for my friends. Yet I remember how hard it was. All around me were different cliques. Kids seemed to hide in them.

Some of the cliques looked out for themselves and stepped on whoever they could in order to climb the "popularity ladder." Then there were those who didn't get noticed much—the so-called losers. Then there were a few teens who really tried to make a difference—not by anything they said but just the way that I saw them treat every person equally. Those were the kids whom I wanted to be like.

I made an effort to love every person I met, whether it was the guy on worship team or the girl at school who was the slacker and into drugs. I did my best to see people the way God sees them. I remember saying to myself, "I'm making this decision right now that I don't care if I'm popular, and I don't even care if I get picked on for doing these things."

I decided I wasn't about to hurt people to be popular. My dad really encouraged me. Every morning before I left for school, he'd tell me, "Today be a leader and not a follower. Strive to have an impact on at least one person's life."

I learned that when you stand up for what you believe, sometimes just with your life and not even with words, that everyone will respect you. Some people might not agree, but they'll respect you for having confidence, not to mention a backbone. They'll notice that there's something bigger in your life that you live for.

hunger for holiness

Since we have these promises, dear friends, let us purify ourselves from everything that contaminates body and spirit, perfecting holiness out of reverence for God.

—2 CORINTHIANS 7:1

Holiness. It's one of those words that conjures up images of uptight church ladies in floral dresses. It even brings to mind a long list of rigid, narrow-minded rules that are out of touch with reality—not to mention completely out of reach.

Yet consider this: Scripture says, "Make every effort to live in peace with all men and to be holy; without holiness no one will see the Lord" (Hebrews 12:14).

I (Margie) want to see the Lord. I want to spend eternity with Him. I don't want to miss out on knowing God because I am without holiness. But at times, my life seems to stray far, far away from anything that remotely resembles holiness.

The truth is, no one is born holy—and none of us can fake it by acting holy or thinking holy thoughts. We can't even pursue holiness unless God stirs that desire in our lives.

So what's a weak, imperfect Christian to do?

Popular author Oswald Chambers also wrestled

with this question. In his book *My Utmost for His Highest*, he writes: "If Jesus Christ is going to regenerate me, what is the problem He faces? It is simply this—I have a heredity in which I had no say or decision; I am not holy, nor am I likely to be; and if all Jesus Christ can do is tell me that I must be holy, His teaching only causes me to despair. But if Jesus Christ is truly a regenerator, someone who can put His own heredity of holiness into me, then I can begin to see what He means when He says that I have to be holy."[7]

• • •

Each morning, I leave my house ready to face a new day—yet before I reach my destination, I find myself confronted with a multitude of choices. (Some are seemingly innocent.)

Do I take the shortcut on "Worldly Wisdom Street" or pursue the longer, more difficult route on "All-That-Really-Matters Avenue"?

I make the choice to turn on Worldly Wisdom Street and strangely enough find myself beginning to linger and listen to the chatter of a thousand voices. I'm drawn to a new perspective—a new way of thinking. I start to buy into the strategies for becoming rich, powerful, beautiful, and famous—goals everyone should strive for, right? My spiritual eyes and ears are becoming dulled as I begin to believe the wisdom of the world.

As I continue to travel down this path, my past subtly sneaks up on my present and begins reminding me of just how unholy I've been.

Guilt. Failures. Hopelessness. Sin. Falling down—getting up. "How holy is that?" the enemy whispers.

Suddenly, the world's smoke and stench of unholy ways swirls around me and begins to cling to my flesh. A Scripture comes to mind, " 'Their sins and lawless acts I will remember no more' " (Hebrews 10:17).

I remind the enemy, "My Father says He doesn't remember."

I shake the world off and go back to the place where I detoured the wrong way. As I turn on All-That-Really-Matters Avenue, the revelation of the Word speaks to me: "For he chose us in him before the creation of the world to be holy and blameless in his sight. In love he predestined us to be adopted as his sons through Jesus Christ, in accordance with his pleasure and will" (Ephesians 1:4–5).

Life does not revolve around me. My desires, my plans, my self-gratifying nature must die. Life is all about His cross and our love for Him.

"As obedient children, do not conform to the evil desires you had when you lived in ignorance. But just as he who called you is holy, so be holy in all you do; for it is written: 'Be holy, because I am holy' " (1 Peter 1:14–16).

I want to be holy. I desire to be holy in all I do. He would not ask me to be holy without providing everything I need to please Him. I must be totally dependent on Him. I cannot rely on myself in any way. I must surrender to Him.

"Once you were alienated from God and were enemies in your minds because of your evil behavior. But now he has reconciled you by Christ's physical body through death to present you holy in his sight, without blemish and free from accusation" (Colossians 1:21–22).

I hunger for His holiness. The hunger becomes a passion to pursue His holiness. I want His holiness to be poured over my head and stream over my soul like honey.

I do not want holiness for my own personal gain. I want to be holy, act holy, and think holy thoughts to please Him and Him alone. My holiness came by way of His cross. He breathes holiness into my life. He will present me holy to the Father. His holiness makes me holy.

"Therefore, I urge you, brothers, in view of God's mercy, to offer your bodies as living sacrifices, holy and pleasing to God—this is your spiritual act of worship" (Romans 12:1).

A FAITH THAT BREATHES

. . . *never tries to earn its way into heaven.* It just *cannot* be done. *Nothing* you do, including "good" works, can protect you from the burning flame of God's holiness. Imagine putting on your rattiest clothes to go fight a fire. That's kind of what Isaiah had in mind when he wrote, "All our righteous acts are like filthy rags; we all shrivel up like a leaf, and like the wind our sins sweep us away" (Isaiah 64:6).

. . . *trusts Christ and what He accomplished by His death and resurrection.* Put yourself in the place of a firefighter for a moment. These courageous men and women have intellectual knowledge that their suits will protect them, but it takes faith and trust to actually step into the flames. It's the same with your Christian faith. You can intellectually know everything there is to know about the Bible, but until you put all your trust in what it says, it's just that—head knowledge. Until you put on the "suit" and step out in faith, you're not protected.

NATALIE LaRUE
Reaching Up to Him

My brother Phillip and I have been inspired by A. W. Tozer's *The Knowledge of the Holy,* St. Augustine's prayers, and various hymns—songs that express deep truths about God. In fact, we recorded "Trinity"—a tune that is our attempt to sing about this awesome mystery. We sing about the wonder of something that we don't understand. In this song, we say that the very thing we can't fathom is the very thing that saves lives.

That's the way it is with God. He simply cannot be grasped by our mortal minds. God is God.

Although God is a mystery to mankind, our hearts yearn to know Him and to serve Him. We strive to be better people and to do good—not because we want to be better than the world but because we long to be like Christ.

Tozer says, "I can do no more justice to the awesome wonder-filled theme called love than a child can grasp a star. Still, by reaching toward the star the child may call attention to it and even indicate the direction one might look to see it. So, as I stretch my heart toward the high, shining love of God, someone who has not before known about it may be encouraged to look up and have hope."

I have come to a place where I don't even want to imagine my life without Christ. And it's beyond just the Lord saving me from hell—it's the daily dependency I have for Him. Every day I see that there's a desperate need for God beyond simply salvation. Despite the mysteries of God, I don't even want to attempt to imagine where I'd be without Him. I know I'd be lost. It makes one quite humble to realize how frail we are in light of God's goodness and strength. Yet it's something that gives us comfort.

accountability — woman to woman

Therefore, since we are surrounded by such a great cloud
of witnesses, let us throw off everything that hinders and
the sin that so easily entangles, and let us run with perse-
verance the race marked out for us. Let us fix our eyes on
Jesus, the author and perfecter of our faith, who for the
joy set before him endured the cross, scorning its shame,
and sat down at the right hand of the throne of God.
Consider him who endured such opposition from sinful
men, so that you will not grow weary and lose heart.

—HEBREWS 12:1–3

I (Tess) have always been surrounded by extraordinary
women. As a girl, I had my mother, a healthy dose
of Nancy Drew, and a whole string of praying saints.
In college, I had some nurturing friends—women like
Karen, Peggy, and Joanie (people who watched me molt
layer upon layer of ill-conceived notions and naiveté
and burst forth into my newly found adulthood like a
stone from a slingshot).

But today, as a grown-up who's well into my career,
I've somehow lost the sweetness of female companionship.

I've found myself relating more to men than is probably good for me. And to be honest, I've even begun taking on the characteristics of independence and self-sufficiency. What happened to the soft lines and the squishy parts of my heart?

I'm too busy providing for myself and standing on my own two feet—living up to my "career potential."

"I don't need girlfriends," I convince myself, "because most of them are skinnier, prettier, and more self-assured than I am." At times, I catch myself being too insecure to stand in their shadow. *Better to stand alone in my own sunlight.*

Recently, though, I started praying about having more accountability and balance in my life. I am tired of having tunnel vision about who I am, where I'm going in my life, and what I feel God is doing. As a result of this time of soul-searching, I developed my own "board of directors," a group of people I trust to hold me accountable.

My board of directors has not remained static but has had a slightly shifting membership as God has placed people into my life. I have at least one married couple on my board; the remainder are a mix of male and female members. We meet at least once a year—or more often, depending on the issues in my life—to discuss and pray over what God is doing.

I prepare for this day by asking God who should be invited. Then I prepare a list of topics and "life issues" I need to share. This range of topics might be as specific as prayer covering, say, a trip to Scotland or as broad as an improvement in my financial acumen. One thing's for sure: I can't run away from any issues, and the board sticks with me until they are prayed through!

Each member receives a copy of the list and each item is prayed over. Then members of my board are allowed to ask questions or give me feedback about what they see in my attitudes or behaviors that might complicate the issue. Relationships, hurts, wounds, desires, dreams, and victories are very specifically talked about, and no probing question is out-of-bounds. They are allowed to be as gentle or firm or direct as they need to be. They ask strong questions, and I give them permission to point out any place where they feel I am rationalizing or have entered into self-deception. And they do!

Then we pray again and ask God to give us all His perspective and to help us know the truth and speak the truth in love. Usually, it is at this point that God speaks to my heart strongly about what the truth of the issue is for me, what's going on in my heart, and what needs to be done about it. And, usually, the Lord confirms His word to me through the post-prayer feedback from my board members. Sometimes, it is just the Lord speaking to me, and I share with them what I feel He is saying to my heart, and they can bear witness with me or expound upon the word with insight or Scripture. Everything is done in a spirit of true love, honor, and respect.

My job is to listen, to keep my heart open to the Holy Spirit's voice, and to receive truth from my friends and weigh it against my knowledge of God's Word and His character. Because I only choose people I feel God has led me to choose and because those people are ones who have proven themselves to be trustworthy with confidences, who practice intercession, and behave with wisdom and discernment, I have little to fear with regard to being led astray. Like the Bereans spoken of in Acts 17:11, we search the Word and measure all things by it.

This group has been a lifesaver for me at times. I have seven people who love me, are committed to me and are praying for me, who ask me how I'm doing with certain issues, and who keep my confidence with very delicate matters. This knowledge works to keep fear and deception away from my door, and I know I never walk alone.

A couple of years ago, the Lord spoke to me and suggested that I begin to seek out relationships with married women. My pastor had begun encouraging us as a congregation to form "life transformation groups" of two or three. These groups would serve as accountability partners and intercessors for one another. Each week, we would meet to ask questions about our thought lives, fantasies, behavior, and temptations and share concerns and victories in a completely honest and confidential manner. Johanna, a mother of four and the wife of a brother in Christ, sought me out, and we have been precious friends. This past year, God has also added Cathy to our LTG. Since then, two of my godly girlfriends have gotten married, and their presence in my life has made a big difference in the way I see and judge myself.

• • •

To whom are you accountable? I highly recommend

having a life transformation partner (or partners) or a "board of directors." It will revolutionize your life and bring a wisdom and security that you have never known before and bring great glory to God out of a transformed life and relationships.

A FAITH THAT BREATHES

. . . *believes that we are our brother's (and sister's) keeper.* Oswald Chambers: "Has it ever dawned on you that you are responsible for other souls spiritually before God? For instance, if I allow any private deflection from God in my life, everyone about me suffers. . . When once you allow physical selfishness, mental slovenliness, moral obtuseness, spiritual density, everyone belonging to your crowd will suffer. 'But,' you say, 'who is sufficient for these things if you erect a standard like that?' Our sufficiency is of God, and of Him alone."[8]

. . . *is real with God—and with others.* The scriptures tell us that God does not want us to be superficial—in our relationship with Him, with others, or in our private lives. In Psalm 51:6, David writes, "Surely you desire truth in the inner parts; you teach me wisdom in the inmost place."

REBECCA ST. JAMES
Accountability Is the Key

Here's something that God has placed on my heart lately: It's important to be mentored. This, of course, goes hand in hand with prayer, Bible reading, and plugging into church.

So, what's mentoring really all about? (Too many Christians just don't get it.) It's a lot like accountability, yet it goes a step further. A mentor offers. . .

> friendship.
> wisdom.
> discipline.
> trustworthy counsel.

I have a mentor, a mature Christian lady who lives in Florida. We talk regularly on the phone—about everything! Here's how this relationship differs from accountability: I seek counsel from my mentor, and I follow her advice. You see, a mentor must be wiser and more mature than you. After all, the whole point is spiritual growth. A mentor is someone who has gone before you and who is willing to challenge you and offer encouragement and who is willing to correct you.

My mom and dad have been really big mentors in my life, too. I think if you have parents who are committed to Jesus and who are really living their faith, then you've got a natural mentoring relationship right in your family.

Want to grow your faith? Want to stand radically for God? Silly questions—of course you do! My advice is this: Seek out a solid mentor. But let me stress a point I made earlier. Along with mentoring, we must pray daily, spend time in the Bible, attend church—and do everything we can to keep our focus on God, not on ourselves.

And here's yet another spiritual growth booster: Hang out with friends who are like-minded. . .friends who are encouragers. . .friends who make knowing and serving God a priority.

a woman
of beauty

myth no. 1: beauty is skin deep

> Your beauty should not come from outward
>
> adornment. . . . It should be that of your inner self,
>
> the unfading beauty of a gentle and quiet spirit,
>
> which is of great worth in God's sight.
>
> —1 PETER 3:3–4

In the past few years, reality TV has become one of the more popular forms of television entertainment. Though the competitions may vary, one common thread runs through each program: The majority of contestants are youthful and physically fit.

A quick scan of the females on these shows reveals a group of women who could just as well appear in the next Miss America pageant. Each girl is prettier than the next, with a flowing mane of hair, flawless skin, and gleaming white teeth. Insecurity washes over me (Carrie) when I consider my own less-than-perfect features alongside those flashing across my television screen. In a culture that often equates physical attractiveness with personal value, it is difficult not to compare myself with these impeccable beauties. Yet time and again, my high opinion of these women fades as soon as they open their mouths. Ugly words often tumble from their lips as they use put-downs, cursing, and lies in hopes of succeeding in the reality show world. At times like this, Jesus' words ring truth, reminding me that " 'out of the overflow of the heart the mouth speaks' " (Matthew 12:34).

• • •

The Bible shares the story of Esther, who lived in the Persian Empire during the reign of King Xerxes. Because of Queen Vashti's disrespectful attitudes, the king replaced her and chose Esther as his new queen because she was "lovely in form and features" (Esther 2:7). Though the king's experience with his first wife should have taught him otherwise, he was still looking at beauty from a strictly physical point of view.

What the king did not know was that, besides being a great beauty, Esther was also one of God's chosen people.

When an evil advisor persuaded Xerxes to issue an edict that all Jews in the land must be destroyed, Esther boldly chose to take action on behalf of her people. One problem: It would be illegal for Esther to go to the king without an invitation. Esther knew that making her request that he spare the Jews could prompt him to call for her death. She knew that going before the king would require careful preparation.

Surprisingly, Esther did not spend her days of preparation undergoing elaborate beauty treatments.

Although she had won the king's favor through her external beauty, she did not call on this feature to appeal for her now.

Instead, Esther focused on her heart. She humbled herself before the Lord, seeking His favor on behalf of the Jews. She spent three days without eating or drinking and asked all the Jews of the city of Susa to join in the fast. Esther's response to the situation was to tend to the spiritual not the physical.

At the end of the three days, Esther must have appeared tired and weak from her lack of nourishment. Yet internally, Esther's beauty must have been shining as never before. In the glow of this radiant spirit, Esther prepared two banquets for the king, during which she calmly presented her request. Xerxes looked upon Esther's act of service favorably and granted her petition that the Jews be saved. God had worked on the king's heart so that Esther's internal beauty outshone her external loveliness.

As the apostle Peter expressed it more than five hundred years later: "Your beauty should not come from outward adornment. . . . Instead, it should be that of your inner self, the unfading beauty of a gentle and quiet spirit, which is of great worth in God's sight" (1 Peter 3:3–4).

Esther's actions show that she understood this principle long before Peter put pen to paper. We can think of Esther as the first true reality "beauty queen"—both inside and out!

A FAITH THAT BREATHES

. . .*doesn't focus solely on external beauty and neglect internal beauty.* Ask God to help you bring balance into this area of your life.

. . .*strives for "perfect submission."* Pray that He will show you specific areas that are in need of submission to Him.

. . .*strives to have a heart for God.* Ask Him to replace self-will and selfish attitudes with a heart that's willing to seek and respond to His will. As much as you desire to grow in the area of internal beauty, God desires it even more!

KIM HILL
Getting Below the Surface

I felt like a volcano ready to erupt. It was my first year of junior high, and I was a new face in a new school. I simply did not know how to fit in. As a Christian, I faced tremendous pressure to be a sweet, quiet girl who always said the right things at just the right times—you know, the prim and proper kind who was liked by everyone. But deep inside was a tug-of-war. A zany tomboy desperately wanted to crawl out.

When a group finally opened up to me, I knew I couldn't hang with them. These kids cussed and smoked and didn't share my values. For the first time in my life, I was challenged with not going along with the crowd and walking the way everyone else did.

Looking back at those difficult days, I remember that I was quickly labeled as a "goodie-goodie Christian." That's when I went through a rude awakening: We spend too much time focusing on outside appearances and not getting below the surface.

Yet the truth is, beauty is much more than skin deep.

It has only been in the past few years that I've learned to be myself. Even when I first stepped on the stage as a singer, I didn't know how to express myself. Today, I'm learning to dig deeper, to be real, and to communicate truth. After all, being a Christian doesn't mean that everything's going to be perfect. So why does each song have to have a happy ending? Life involves questions, and the great thing about being a Christian is that we have found the Source of real hope.

Sharing the hope of Christ has been my mission as a musician. I admit that stripping away the false fronts and stepping out as the real person God intends takes confidence.

But trust God. He'll give it to you. Trust me—I know this from experience.

Above all, dig deep. Get way below the surface to the rich treasure God has for you.

myth no. 2: only Mary Kay does makeovers

Your beauty should not come from outward adornment,
such as braided hair and the wearing of gold jewelry and
fine clothes. Instead, it should be that of your inner self,
the unfading beauty of a gentle and quiet spirit,
which is of great worth in God's sight.

—1 PETER 3:3–4

I (Vanessa) have been a Mary Kay representative for the past few years, and I do makeovers. I must admit, I love being a beauty consultant. But I have been serving Jesus Christ for many more years, and I am even more convinced that nothing in life is more important than knowing Him personally. A growing, intimate relationship with Him is just what the soul cries out for.

Beauty comes in all kinds of packages. Growing up as a timid, unpopular, and even picked-on young girl, I was full of insecurities. I couldn't help thinking that all the pretty girls were the ones everyone valued. I would search for some affirmation from my family and my peers, asking how I could change myself to fit in—to be a little more accepted. Often, I got the same advice:

"Just be yourself."

I hated those words. How could that advice possibly help?

In all honesty, I *was* myself—yet being *me* apparently wasn't good enough. I felt as if the world was looking for beauty and that I always came up short. I simply did not want to be myself. I wanted to be "the other girl"—the pretty face everyone loved and esteemed.

As a young lady, I desperately needed real love—perfect love.

I dreamed of finding someone who would love me completely even when they knew me completely. I longed to know someone who would never reject me, despite my imperfections. I never again wanted to wear a mask, attempting to hide the person I truly was inside.

Is there someone out there who will accept me no matter how many times I do something stupid, or forget something important, or publicly put my foot in my mouth? I'd often ask myself.

I wanted a friend who would look at me and see *me*—not the clothes or the hair or any of the other "skin-deep" stuff.

This dilemma persisted during my youth. Then I met the person I had always longed to know. I found someone who loved me more than I could ever imagine. I found Christ.

My outlook gradually began to change. Day by day, the truth began to fill me as I learned to look full in the face of my Creator.

•••

When I gave my life to Jesus, things changed. Actually, let me rephrase that: *Things* didn't really change—but *I* changed.

I discovered that I was popular with Him. I found that He really did like me and that I didn't have to put on a show. And a wonderful thing began to happen: I discovered that as I began to know Him, I began to know myself. I wasn't the young lady everyone else said I was. I no longer saw myself through the eyes of cold, judgmental peers. To God, I wasn't too short, too skinny, too shy, or too slow. I didn't always have to say all the right words—or feel the pressure of being witty or smart or following the latest trends.

With God, I was loved—and I knew I was loved. And to this day, I still know it.

These days, I love playing around with cosmetics. I try to take good care of my skin and hair. I think it's fun. I love trying on all the new colors that come out and getting together with my friends to check out the latest blushes and lipsticks. There's no pressure to look perfect or to live up to some impossible image, so I can truly enjoy it now.

I love makeovers. But underneath the mascara and lipstick and cool clothes is a happy heart—a heart made free and clean and beautiful by the One who created it, my Lord and Savior.

He is the person I look for now when I look into a mirror every morning. And you know what? He is always there. The changes Christ has made in the deepest part of me are exactly what people really see when they look into my eyes. They see Christ in me when they look at my smile or hear my voice. And as long as I keep myself in the center of His will, I will be full of Him—full of His beauty.

A FAITH THAT BREATHES

. . .never substitutes the world's lies for God's truth. As a Christian—when you go to the movies and watch TV—your heart should feel saddened by the so-called popular "perfect" people who may never discover what Jesus really thinks of them. As followers of Jesus, we should spend time every day, thanking God for the incredible change He has made in us. We know now how to really live.

. . .knows that Mary Kay does great makeovers—but they are only skin deep. The real change is made by our Master. It is deep and permanent. He will make a change that is sweet and beautiful and free. And He will perfect everything we willingly surrender to Him. It is always a change that lasts forever.

KRISTIN SWINFORD (ZOEGIRL)

You're Not a "Plain Jane"

Self-confidence is one of the biggest issues that we've come across on the road. It's usually something we hear from girls while talking, praying, and counseling with them.

The truth is, way too many Christian ladies deal with this issue. They fall into the trap of thinking they have no friends and feeling as if they don't measure up. And everywhere they go, they're bombarded with the message that beauty is everything. Just walk past magazine racks and count the headlines that promise "Ten Steps to a Perfect Body." Our whole culture is way too focused on outward beauty.

I have to be honest and admit that even ZOEgirl has been airbrushed on some of our album covers—despite spending hours in makeup and having our hair done.

Yet while the world demands that we look perfect, God communicates a different message.

As His creations, we are worth so much to Him. God loves us for who we are and who He made us to be. We don't have to find our self-worth in beauty products or boyfriends. God looks at us differently. He sees beauty and worth and greatness in us—even when we can't comprehend it.

And He gives real makeovers—the kind that come from the inside out. The kind that changes hearts and transforms souls.

We've recorded a song titled "Dismissed." It communicates that we have the power to dismiss the things in our lives that are negative—whether they're vices, bad habits, or so-called friends who pull us down.

We have the power to "not go there" and to turn away from the world's lies. The Bible says that whatever we ask in the name of Jesus will be done; therefore, we have the power to dismiss those negative influences in our lives.

myth no. 3: you can have it all

For who knows what is good for a man in life, during
the few and meaningless days he passes through like a
shadow? Who can tell him what will happen under
the sun after he is gone? . . . Now all has been heard;
here is the conclusion of the matter: Fear God and keep
his commandments, for this is the whole duty of man.
For God will bring every deed into judgment,
including every hidden thing, whether it is good or evil.

—ECCLESIASTES 6:12, 12:13–14

My mother was right. It's often hard for daughters to admit this, isn't it? But it's true—she's quite a wise woman. When I (Tiffany) was younger, I spent far too many hours watching television. There were times my mom would walk in the room, turn off the tube, and demand that I go outside and find something else to do. She knew that I'd benefit from the fresh air and sunlight—and that engaging in physical activity and using my imagination was good for a growing girl.

My mom also knew that allowing TV commercials

to bombard my senses with unreal expectations and materialistic philosophies wasn't healthy for an impressionable kid. (Besides, they gave me lots of "wants" to add to my already long Christmas and birthday wish lists!) Okay, I'll say it one last time—she was right!

To this day, I can still recall dozens of TV jingles. I'll bet it's the same for you. Go ahead—test yourself. When you hear the following words, do you automatically start to hum the tune? (Be honest.)

"I can bring home the bacon, fry it up in a pan, and never ever let you forget you're a man. 'Cause I'm a woman. . ."

And when it comes to this particular TV commercial, it's far more than just another jingle that's stuck in our brains. The message behind it is actually what many women are trying to live up to. It has become our unspoken motto. Translation: Simultaneously having a successful career, cooking delicious meals, taking care of the house, being sexy, and maintaining a healthy romantic relationship is all possible because "I'm a woman." Not Superwoman—just a mere woman.

I get exhausted just thinking about living up to all of these expectations in a single day, every day—yet I find myself trying to do it.

As I look around, I realize that I'm not alone. Women, in general, are trying to have it all. And we are all so busy that we are missing out on life. True, we're getting a lot accomplished. But we're not *experiencing* life in the process.

We race to work, our minds exploding with a million

other thoughts: *Which birthday gift should I buy my boss? Will I meet my deadlines today? I hope my husband likes frozen meatloaf!*

We cook dinner, wondering if there is enough gas in the lawn mower. We attend a meeting at work—while paying bills in our head. We take our kids to the park *and* make a mental shopping list for our stop at the grocery store on the way home.

Most women have taken multitasking and time management to the extreme. Each of these goals is positive and worthy of our effort. The problem arises when we expect to achieve all of them at the same time. The truth is, we need to give ourselves a break.

During a conference for women, popular speaker and author Kay Cole James once commented, "I can have it all, but not all at the same time."

After hearing this simple and profound remark, I began to look at success with a fresh perspective. I stopped and assessed my life and my goals. I systematically examined and prioritized every element. What a relief!

I stopped allowing someone else's expectations to drive my daily agenda. And in this spirit of freedom, I made some life-changing decisions. It was not an abandonment of responsibility, just an adjustment of priorities. With a little mental discipline, I began living in the moment.

Life is demanding and requires a lot of prayer and planning. But as we allow God into our daily lives and schedules, He will guide our daily steps as we move toward the future.

A FAITH THAT BREATHES

. . . *knows that whatever we value most gets our time and energy.* How does this play out with your faith? Is spending time with God a daily priority? Or is He getting squeezed out of your busy schedule?

. . . *finds rest in Christ's arms.* Consider praying this prayer: "Lord Jesus, I need time alone with You. Help me to make my faith a priority. I need time to give You my undivided attention, time to listen, time to let go, time to find rest for my weariness. Lord, help me to fall into Your arms daily. Amen."

NATALIE LARUE
Will We Ever Be Satisfied?

Not one of us will ever be satisfied with who we are. That is, on our own. Yet finding answers to the longings of our hearts is within reach. We can know who we are—and who we were created to be—through God. We can finally realize that God accepts and loves us more than anyone else for exactly who we are. And get this: He is satisfied with who we are.

My brother (and music partner), Phillip, began to understand this truth in the eighth grade—at a point when he grew sick of trying to look cool in front of his friends.

"My so-called friends started putting me down and making fun of me, and it was a really hard time in my life," he said. "When I was at school, I felt out of place and like an outcast. I felt like I had to do something to get noticed and known by others.

"Instead, I did something radical. Because I'd been ignoring God and neglecting my faith, I decided to get back on track with Him. Shortly thereafter, He began to spark in me a desire to minister through music."

Slowly, something amazing began to happen. As he put his focus on knowing and serving God, Phillip began to care less about fitting in with his friends—and less about what the world thought. God not only strengthened his courage, He showed him his true identity in Christ and gave him a vision for the future.

Phillip's healing journey has been an encouragement to me. And here's a passage of Scripture that means a lot to us: Hebrews 3:1–6. Take a look: "Therefore, holy brothers, who share in the heavenly calling, fix your thoughts on Jesus, the apostle and high priest whom we confess. He was faithful to the one who appointed him, just as Moses was faithful in all God's house. Jesus has been found worthy of greater honor than Moses, just as the builder of a house has greater honor than the house itself. For every house is built by someone, but God is the builder of everything. Moses was faithful as a servant in all God's house, testifying to what would be said in the future. But Christ is faithful as a son over God's house. And we are his house, if we hold on to our courage and the hope of which we boast."

•

mending a broken image: part 1

> Though my father and mother forsake me,
> the LORD will receive me. Teach me your way, O LORD;
> lead me in a straight path because of my oppressors.
> Do not turn me over to the desire of my foes,
> for false witnesses rise up against me, breathing out vio-
> lence. I am still confident of this: I will see the goodness
> of the Lord in the land of the living. Wait for the Lord; be
> strong and take heart and wait for the Lord.
>
> —PSALM 27:10–14

"Mirror, mirror on the wall. . .who's the fairest of them all?"

No doubt the child in you remembers the wicked queen's words from the *Snow White* fairytale. The question is, as a young woman, what does your mirror say to you today? Who is that reflection that stares back at you?

Consider this: Each time you look into a mirror, you gaze upon a *two-dimensional* image of yourself. You do not see your complete *self*. The mirror cannot tell you who you are, and it cannot define you.

How would you look if the mirror was cracked and broken? You'd see misshapen, incomplete pieces, right? But if the mirror is broken, does this mean that the reflection you see is a true representation of who you are? Absolutely not.

Yet the truth is—regardless of race, education, or position—women today are using broken mirrors to define themselves. And every time we gaze at an incomplete reflection, we begin to believe half-truths. We convince ourselves that we don't have the grace, the looks, the style, the intelligence, the talent, the money, or the sex appeal that we think we should see reflected in the mirror.

We tell ourselves what we should have:

- the charisma of Britney Spears
- the admiration of Madonna
- the style of Halle Berry
- the talent of Norah Jones
- the sex appeal of Julia Roberts

But the image of the woman we desperately *want to see* reflected in the broken mirror of society is *not God's image of us.* That is not the mirror of truth. In fact, this image is not *real* at all.

So then, why do we buy into these half-truths? Why are we convinced that our broken mirrors show us reality?

• • •

The mirror of society is broken in a million ways, but we keep looking into it, hoping that with just a little more practice, a few more aerobics lessons, a couple of dress sizes smaller, and a bit more psychic contortion, we will be able to see in that mirror the reflection of a woman that makes some sense in a broken world.

As a result, we become human Picasso paintings. We're put together in pieces that don't quite fit yet resemble something human if you cock your head just the right way and shut one eye.

Is this who you are striving to be—a pale reflection of Julia Roberts or perhaps Beyonce Knowles. . .or better yet, Oprah Winfrey? Think about it: Aren't their mirrors broken, too?

Kick that mirror off the wall. Go ahead! Do your best Catwoman impression and kick that broken, filthy piece of lying glass off the wall. Want to know where you can go to see a true reflection of your *self*? Here it is—are you ready?

• " 'For in Him we live and move and have our being. . . . Therefore, since we are the offspring of God, we ought not to think that the Divine Nature is like gold or silver or stone' " (or Julia Roberts, or Oprah Winfrey, or Halle Berry), " 'something shaped by art and man's devising' " (Acts 17:28–29 NKJV, additional comments ours).

- "Grace and peace be multiplied to you in the knowledge of God and of Jesus our Lord, as His divine power has given to us all things that pertain to life and godliness, through the knowledge of Him who called us by glory and virtue, by which have been given to us exceedingly great and precious promises, that through these you may be partakers of the *divine nature*, having escaped the corruption is in the world through lust" (2 Peter 1:2–4 NKJV, emphasis ours).

- "But we all, with unveiled face, beholding as in a mirror the glory of the Lord, are being transformed into the same image from glory to glory, just as by the Spirit of the Lord" (2 Corinthians 3:18 NKJV).

So who are you? If you've entered into a personal, intimate relationship with Jesus Christ—Son of the Living God, Creator of the universe, Savior, Redeemer, King, and the lover of your soul—then there is only one correct answer: You are a daughter of God and a partaker of the divine nature.

Only in *relationship* with Jesus will He show you your true self. Only in relationship with Him will you be transformed into His image. Only by gazing steadfastly into His Word will you see a true reflection of your true self and the world around you.

"Sing, O daughter of Zion! Shout, O Israel! Be glad

and rejoice with all your heart, O daughter of Jerusalem! The LORD has taken away your judgments, He has cast out your enemy. The King of Israel, the LORD, is in your midst; You shall see disaster no more. . . . 'The LORD. . .The Mighty One, will save; He will rejoice over you with gladness, He will quiet you with His Love, He will rejoice over you with singing' " (Zephaniah 3:14–15, 17 NKJV).

Remove the broken mirrors from your house and begin to see your true reflection mirrored in the eyes of the One who loves you best, daughter of God. Gaze into His Word of Truth and come to see who you really are.

A FAITH THAT BREATHES

. . .*takes inventory*. Sometime soon, stand in front of a full-length mirror and evaluate the person you see. As you study the woman in the mirror, ask yourself some honest questions: *Who am I? Is this the best me? Is there room for improvement? What can I change? What must I accept about myself?*

. . .*sees from Christ's perspective.* As you stand in front of the mirror, evaluating yourself, remember this: Reflected in His light of love, you can see your beauty, your intelligence, your loveliness, your gifts, and your true purpose. Only by steadfastly immersing yourself in His "exceedingly great and precious promises" will you become a willing partaker of the divine nature.

. . .seeks to focus on the right image—Christ's. Think about all the other times you've spent in front of mirrors, combing your hair, checking out those new clothes—expending so much effort seeking acceptance. Now consider this: Christ "had no beauty or majesty to attract us to him, nothing in his appearance that we should desire him" (Isaiah 53:2). People were attracted to Jesus because His beauty was internal. His heart emanated unlimited love. The peace in His eyes drew crowds. The joy of His smile was contagious. Seek to make His focus your own.

. . .trusts God with insecurities. Ask the Lord to help you make up for your weaknesses by concentrating on your strengths. In other words, if you're not exactly crazy about your looks, tell yourself this: *So I may not be model material. Big deal—I'm not alone! Besides, my self-worth isn't dependent on the arrangement of my body. I'll put my energy into a skill that'll help me feel good about myself. I'm a talented _____ [insert the word that applies to you, such as musician, artist, athlete]. I'll continue to improve the skills God has given me and use them to serve Him.*

NICHOLE NORDEMAN
Do You See God's Masterpiece in the Mirror?

From the minute we're born, Satan tries to fill our heads with all kinds of deceptions. One of his most popular lies goes something like this: "There is no hope. You are worthless and alone and would be better off just giving up."

Day after day, the enemy tries desperately to trap us in a web of negative thoughts and feelings of loneliness and desperation. Have you been deceived? Can you relate to what I'm saying? If so, I have some good news for you: Jesus Christ is ready to break you free from Satan's lies.

The truth is, our self-worth and value are grounded in our Savior. So during those moments when you feel like a loser—those times when you don't think you're part of the "right" crowd or that you're not making the grade—Jesus says, "You do matter, and your life is valuable because of who you are in Me."

It took me a long time to learn this. As a teen, I tried to find my value in relationships and popularity. I eventually learned that these pursuits are empty. More important, I began to realize that believing Satan's lies can lead to a long series of bad choices that can have some significant consequences.

When you catch yourself being deceived, turn to the truth. Pour out your heart to Jesus in prayer and trust Him.

mending a broken image:
part 2

Praise be to the God and Father of our Lord Jesus Christ,

the Father of compassion and the God of all comfort,

who comforts us in all our troubles,

so that we can comfort those in any trouble with

the comfort we ourselves have received from God.

For just as the sufferings of Christ flow over into our lives,

so also through Christ our comfort overflows.

—2 CORINTHIANS 1:3–5

Are you broken because of bad relationships?

Have you been torn in two by others—then slammed against the rock walls of life? Are you bruised, wounded, hurting? Have you loved the wrong people? Trusted too much? Loved too much? Revealed your heart to extinction?

If it is true that we become "one" with someone with whom we've shared physical intimacy, does it stand to reason that if you've "joined" yourself to more than one person, each time you separate from a relationship, there is spiritually a little less of you left to bring into the next relationship? Have you subconsciously been stumbling from person to person, trying to find your missing pieces and somehow reassemble your heart, your self-esteem, your soul? Have you been giving yourself away, piece by piece, in your pursuit of finding fulfillment in a relationship? Are there men walking around, carrying a part of you with them that you will never get back?

Is it possible that the more you "give yourself away" to men, searching for companionship and "completion," that you actually become less and less your true self? That would be ironic, wouldn't it? We're sure Alanis Morrisette hasn't thought of that one.

How does God mend this? How can God possibly accept us with all our hurts, mistakes, and failures? If we've had trouble making relationships work here on earth, why should we think that a relationship with God would last? In our frailty, brokenness, and humanness, we cry, "Do you still want me?"

The simple answer is, "Yes." Actually, not just "Yes" but "Y-E-E-E-E-E-S-S-S-S-S-S!"

• • •

Our heavenly Father loves us unconditionally. This means that we can mess up, fall down, break the rules, and run away—and even come to Him in pieces. He will accept us because He has loved us since before the foundation of the world. Before we existed, He saw us and loved us. (See Psalm 139.) Before we came into existence, He purchased our salvation. Where formerly there was no path to His presence, we now have a way carved out of the wilderness—straight to His heart.

- "He heals the brokenhearted and binds up their wounds" (Psalm 147:3).

- "He restores my soul; He leads me in the paths of righteousness for His name's sake" (Psalm 23:3 NKJV).

- "Therefore, if anyone is in Christ, he is a new creation; old things have passed away; behold, all things have become new" (2 Corinthians 5:17 NKJV).

- "Now may the God of peace who brought up our Lord Jesus from the dead, that great Shepherd of the sheep, through the blood of the everlasting covenant, make you complete in every good work to do His will, working in you what is well pleasing in His sight, through Jesus Christ, to whom be glory forever and ever" (Hebrews 13:20–21 NKJV).

Men do not complete us. There is only One who has the power to make us the women we were created to be from the beginning—God.

And when God completes us, He doesn't just take the broken pieces and paste them back together so we look like something useful again. Instead, He reclaims our brokenness, our crushed spirit, and takes that finely ground powder, mixing it with the fresh, moist clay of His own spiritual matrix and—with His own hands—begins to lovingly, slowly, and carefully reshape and remold us. He takes from His own Spirit and re-creates us from the inside out. He breathes His breath into us, whispering words of love and life into our souls until we are able to breathe deeply of His life within us—and without so much pain.

Through Jesus, we are Eve restored. We are now free in Jesus to become everything He intended for us to be from the beginning of time—completely free and completely His. We are *remade*.

The Creator teaches us to walk again and to see with new eyes. What was stolen from us or given away, our heavenly Father creates anew. Why would we want our old life?

A FAITH THAT BREATHES

. . . *has renewed hope*. Proverbs 15:4 says, "The tongue that brings healing is a tree of life, but a deceitful tongue crushes the spirit." Begin to replace "I don't know how" with "Now is the time for me to learn." Replace "I can't" with "I will."

. . . *is complete in Christ*. When we become the Bride of Christ and join Him in a holy relationship of service and love, we are clothed in white raiment, the robes of His righteousness. All that was lost is restored in a new way. We become complete in Him and will never be the same again.

. . .is comforted by God's gaze. Has your spirit been broken by shame or by a thousand little hurts, insults, and disappointments? When you look into the broken mirror of society, do you see the perfection it demands of you—the images of Oprah Winfrey, Madonna, Britney Spears, and Halle Berry? (Remember our discussion in yesterday's lesson, Day 18?) This is a society that looks at you and glances away—a society that does not hold your gaze because you can never live up to its reflection of broken perfection. To the world, you are meaningless. Yet to God, you are priceless.

. . .basks in God's gaze. Place your soul in the healing hands of the Father who gazes intently at you and who *never looks away.* He will transform you by the renewing of your mind. He will never stop looking at you. He will never leave you or forsake you. You are His beloved, His Bride, His Body, and His treasure. He won't just *mend* your image, He wants to re-create you in His image.

. . .walks with the wise. Proverbs 13:20 says, "He who walks with the wise grows wise, but a companion of fools suffers harm." In other words, a friend of winners will be a winner, but a friend of fools will die. Now check out 1 Corinthians 15:33–34: "Do not be misled:

'Bad company corrupts good character.' Come back to your senses as you ought, and stop sinning; for there are some who are ignorant of God—I say this to your shame."

REBECCA ST. JAMES

Reach Out to the "God of Second Chances"

I recently had the opportunity to play the role of Mary Magdalene in a rock opera tour called *! HERO*. It was certainly a challenge and even a bit ironic taking on this part. She was a prostitute; I've always taken a stand for faith and purity. But this experience has also given me compassion for her. It's awesome when you realize that Christ came to earth for the "Mary Magdalenes" of this world.

In a duet with Michael Tait—the artist who played Hero [the Messiah] on the tour—my character asks him, "How do you know all this stuff about me? You've never met me before!" Despite her sin, Hero offered her living water—and eternal life.

God gives us all second chances, grace, and forgiveness. Mary Magdalene gives testimony to the transformation that Jesus makes in a life. Regardless of who we are, we've all made mistakes and we've all messed up. We've all sinned. None of us is worthy of God's love. Yet, He offers His grace and forgiveness to us.

Through the years, a lot of people have come up to me after my shows and have shared some truly horrible stories and some very difficult problems. Specifically, one girl told me how she'd slept with her boyfriend. She said that he'd broken up with her right away, which made her want to commit suicide. This young lady ended up sleeping with a whole bunch of different guys and falling into drugs and alcohol.

After she finished talking, I felt led to write on her hand with a Sharpie the words *You are loved*. Then I looked her in the eyes and repeated those words, "You are loved. Don't ever forget this."

I used to share this story during my concerts, and I've had people come up to me afterward saying, "Thank you for that story. Can you write that reminder on my hand, too?"

It's absolutely beautiful how He cleanses us and heals our brokenness. It's absolutely comforting that we have a new life in Him. We have renewed hope in the God of second chances.

the woman God sees

She never left the temple but worshiped
night and day, fasting and praying.

—LUKE 2:37

My husband, Jim, and I (Carrie) recently welcomed our first child into our family. As any expectant mother can testify, the question of what to name the baby is a popular topic of discussion in the months leading up to the birth. When an ultrasound revealed that our child would be a girl, Jim and I began searching in earnest for the right name.

It was important to us to choose a name that would guide us in praying for our daughter. As we considered the examples of women from the Bible, we were drawn to the story of Anna.

• • •

Anna was a widowed prophetess who was already eighty-four years old when Jesus was born. In his gospel, Luke tells us that Anna spent all of her waking hours praying, fasting, and worshiping in the temple. When Joseph and Mary brought baby Jesus to the temple to dedicate Him to the Lord, God allowed Anna to recognize Jesus as the Savior: "She gave thanks to God and spoke about the child to all who were looking forward to the redemption of Jerusalem" (Luke 2:38).

I love this story because it reminds me of the faithfulness of God. Anna had been married for only seven years before her husband died. Though we don't know how old she was when she married, we can safely guess that she had spent the majority of her life as a widow. Most likely, this isn't how Anna had envisioned her life would play out. Had I walked in the shoes of that young bride, I would have wrestled with disappointment in God, asking: "Didn't He see that my hopes and plans for the future had been destroyed? In fact, did He even see me at all?"

All of us want to be seen by God—to have assurance that He knows exactly what is happening in our lives, that He cares about us, and that He is intimately involved in our circumstances. Scripture doesn't fill us in on all that occurred in Anna's life from the time that she became a widow until the time she reached her eighty-fourth birthday. All the same, the facts indicate that if Anna felt bitterness, she invited God to purify her heart so that she could again trust that He *did* see her. How else could she have dedicated her life wholeheartedly to the worship of God?

The perfect "payoff" of Anna's story sends shivers up my spine. Anna spent decades living a life that praised God. Her reward for believing that God saw *her* was to be honored by seeing *God*. If we are Christians, we have the hope of seeing God at the end of our lives on this earth. Anna was one of the privileged few who was blessed to see God face-to-face in this world.

More than thirty years after Anna's encounter with Jesus, our Lord spoke to a large crowd on a hillside. As He taught, He shared about the attitudes of the heart that God blesses. I can't help but wonder if Jesus had a picture of Anna in His mind's eye as He spoke. " 'Blessed are the pure in heart, for they will see God' " (Matthew 5:8).

Each night, I pray for my daughter Anna before I put her to bed. I pray that my Anna would have the same heart as the biblical Anna. I ask God that she would live a pure and worshipful life that He would see with pleasure. I ask, too, that she would know the ultimate joy of seeing His face.

A FAITH THAT BREATHES

. . .is committed to a daily quiet time. In today's society, Anna's example seems impossible and impractical. She might have been free to spend all day and night worshiping in the temple, but many of us find it challenging to be faithful in keeping our daily quiet time with God. The demands of school, work, or caring for a family fill our schedules; the addition of time with friends, exercise, or running errands packs our schedules to overflowing. Despite our hectic lifestyle, our passion for quiet time must make it a priority.

. . .maintains a heart like Anna's. How can we do this in our fast-paced lives? One idea from the Bible is to "be joyful always; pray continually; give thanks in all circumstances, for this is God's will for you in Christ Jesus" (1 Thessalonians 5:16–18). Fortunately, God sees us wherever we are. We don't have to be inside a church building in order for Him to take notice of us. This means we can lift our hearts to Him at any moment throughout the day. While preparing our breakfast, or sitting at a stoplight, or folding laundry—any of these times are perfect for turning our thoughts to our heavenly Father and speaking a word of prayer or praise to Him.

. . .strives to lift up our immediate circumstances to Him. This often happens when we pray during the routine parts of our day, instead of saving it all up for a bedtime marathon prayer in which we try to remember all that we wanted to share with God from our day. Plus, when we talk to God throughout our day, we can be encouraged by remembering that He hears—and sees—us all day long, whenever we turn to Him.

. . .is comforted by the truth that we are daughters of God. We are invited to come boldly into the throne room of our Father, to dine at His

table and partake of His divine nature and free gifts. For He has given us everything we need for life and godliness. We are highly valued and precious in His sight. He places a crown on our head and lifts our countenance.

BARLOWGIRL
You Have Perfect Value in God's Eyes

"It's okay to be different—because you have perfect value in God's eyes!" This is the message BarlowGirl is sharing through their all-girl rock band. And for these three sisters—Alyssa, Lauren, and Becca Barlow—the word *conformity* isn't even in their vocabulary. When BarlowGirl made their national debut with Superchic[k], the band was so impressed with the Barlow girls' outlook on purity that they penned a song about the trio, aptly titled "Barlow Girls." In the paragraphs that follow, Alyssa, Lauren, and Becca share their thoughts on image, beauty, and their quest to live genuinely as the women God sees.

Alyssa on "The Woman God Sees"

As girls, we're constantly looking in the mirror. And even though we know we're made in God's image, it's funny how we forget this truth when we gaze at our reflection—we're often so critical of who we see.

Yet my sisters and I have made a conscious effort, when we look in the mirror, to say, "I don't have to be who you're telling me I should be. You're telling me I should look like these models, but I know when I look in the mirror that everything is as it should be because I am made by God."

If you haven't done so already, check out our song on this subject called (you guessed it) "Mirror."

Lauren on "Feelings vs. Truth"

A friend came to us and said, "I'm really struggling with my walk with God. I talk to Him, and I cry out to Him, but it feels as if He never hears me. He never answers my prayers. It really feels as if God has turned His back on me."

To be honest, we have felt this way at times in our own lives, too. But this is the truth we cling to (and what we shared with our friend): We simply have to trust that God is with us, whether or not we can feel His presence. In the Bible, He promises that He will never leave us or forsake us. He loves us and values us.

Becca on "The Lord's Transforming Hope"

Striving to be "good Christian girls" as teenagers, we constantly felt the pressure to have the right answers for everything. But now that we're more mature, we've concluded that having all the right answers will not help us. Right answers don't change your heart or even make you a better person. Our only hope is in God changing our hearts.

Here's a verse that sums up this truth: "Do not conform any longer to the pattern of this world, but be transformed by the renewing of your mind. Then you will be able to test and approve what God's will is—his good, pleasing and perfect will" (Romans 12:2).

the woman God uses

Blessed is the man who does not walk in the counsel of the
wicked or stand in the way of sinners or sit in the seat of
mockers. But his delight is in the law of the LORD,
and on his law he meditates day and night.
He is like a tree planted by streams of water,
which yields its fruit in season and whose leaf does not
wither. Whatever he does prospers.

—PSALM 1:1–3

There were two sisters who lived in the same house. Both knew Jesus and loved Him and called Him their dearest friend and Lord, yet they had very different priorities. Then one day Jesus came to visit. That's right, the Lord came to Mary and Martha's home!

Upon His arrival, the polarization of the two sisters became clear. Martha went straight to the kitchen to prepare the meal, while Mary sat at Jesus' feet and listened to Him speak. While Martha cooked and cleaned, Mary focused on grasping Jesus' words. While Martha worked, Mary worshiped. While Martha hurried around, tackling her to-do list, Mary was preoccupied with only one thing—her relationship with the Lord.

Martha's work was important, of course, but it was not the most important thing at that moment. She was so busy that she had no time to sit at the feet of the Lord and receive His love, fellowship, and wisdom. Finally, He spoke to her and gently corrected her priorities: " 'Martha, Martha. . .you are worried and upset about many things, but only one thing is needed. Mary has chosen what is better, and it will not be taken away from her' " (Luke 10:41–42).

• • •

It's all about priorities. Before God's people are able to serve, they must spend time at His feet drawing from His strength.

Busyness is a universal problem. It happens to the best of us. Our lives are so jam-packed with competing priorities that there is little time to stop and receive the strength that the Lord is waiting to give. Moses, the spiritual leader of Israel, was once preoccupied with judging the affairs of his people. He poured almost all of his energy into their lives, preparing them to serve God. He had so many good and honorable tasks to complete, yet it was far too much for just one person. Until the day his father-in-law, Jethro, stepped in with some loving advice: " 'The work is too heavy for you; you cannot handle it alone. Listen now to me and I will give you some advice, and may God be with you. You must be the people's representative before God and bring their disputes to him' " (Exodus 18:18–19).

From the God-inspired guidance of his father-in-law,

Moses created a unique justice system that included a hierarchy of judges trained to handle disputes and criminal crimes. The more demanding cases would work their way through the higher courts and then to Moses. The people's needs were met, and Moses was free to spend more time listening to God's counsel and direction. From then on, the Scriptures portray Moses as a man who sought God's strength daily, and he was able to move out and better serve and teach the people.

God's people must delight themselves in His strength before they can step out and serve effectively. Mary, Moses, King David, and Joshua are a few of the many examples of this principle found in the Scriptures. And better yet is the life of Jesus as He walked the earth. "Very early in the morning, while it was still dark, Jesus got up, left the house and went off to a solitary place, where he prayed" (Mark 1:35).

Jesus arose in the morning seeking the heart of His Father. He desired this time of fellowship and worship. He took advantage of one of the few times He was alone—early in the morning. It was so important to Him that He willingly gave up sleep and quiet time in order to spend quality time with His Father. He knew that soon His hectic day would kick in and the crowds, His disciples, and the demands of the day would crowd in on Him. He also knew that He needed the sustaining strength and love of His Father above.

Is Jesus speaking your name? Is He calling out to you? Why don't you come and worship at His feet?

. . . *prepares daily for service in God's kingdom.* The Creator of the universe desires our attention. He wants to hear our thoughts and fears, guide us through the day, heal our bodies or our broken hearts, hold us tight, and let us know that we are loved. Make the decision to draw from the Eternal Source before you set out on your daily mission.

. . . *asks the Lord to realign our priorities.* When it comes to your faith in Christ, where are your priorities? Is having a deeper, more committed relationship with Jesus your No. 1 passion? When you make mistakes, do you confess them to Jesus, asking Him to transform your heart? Or is sin driving a wedge between you and God? And could it be that other priorities are filling your heart—friends, guys, school, a job, entertainment choices, materialistic pursuits? Spend some time in prayer, asking God to realign your priorities. Ask Him to transform you into a woman He can use.

KELLY MINTER

Wrestling with Angels

Often in life we want certain things and spend our time striving for these things. All the while, the Lord wants to give us something much grander. And sometimes, as Christians, we're guilty of boxing ourselves in. But the person God uses has learned to leave behind preconceived notions. (I've recorded a song on this topic called "Open Up the Sky.")

The Lord wants us to reach past the limits and confess our own thinking. Too often, we get caught up in our own dreams and miss the greater picture around us.

On my album *Wrestling with Angels,* the title cut tells the story of Jacob. After wrestling through the night with the angel of the Lord, he bravely breathed the words, "I will not let you go until you bless me." Jacob was willing to stay in the fight and wrestle through the night because he knew that whatever blessing the Lord had for him was worth the wait and worth the fight. In the end, he walked away with a limp—a changed and different person.

This is how I want to walk away from all my encounters with the Lord. And if wrestling and limping and struggling are the means by which I can take hold of Him and His blessings, then I am honored to take these hard steps.

It's expensive to live for Jesus. It requires a lot of sacrifices when it comes to putting Him at the forefront of our lives. Yet this is what's required from the kind of woman He chooses to use.

a woman
of purity

passion for purity

> Do you not know that your body is a temple of the Holy
> Spirit, who is in you, whom you have received from God?
> You are not your own; you were bought at a price.
> Therefore honor God with your body.
>
> —1 CORINTHIANS 6:19–20

The day Michael asked me (Tiffany) to marry him was both the beginning of a wonderful journey together and the culmination of thousands of moments he and I had already spent together.

It was Christmas Eve 1996, and Michael and I had spent the afternoon hiking in the wilderness near my parents' home in Pineville, West Virginia.

"This is my favorite spot," I said as we reached the end of the trail—a steep ridge with a postcard-perfect view. "I used to come here when I had big decisions to make."

"I can see why," Michael agreed. "This place definitely feels a little closer to God."

Rugged mountains and misty groves of oak and spruce stretched endlessly across the West Virginia landscape. It didn't take a bolt of lightning to convince Michael that the setting was ideal and the moment was right.

Although this special moment was filled with

jitters and emotion, several key things had given us confidence: Michael and I had built our relationship on a foundation of. . .

Faith. Jesus and His will for our lives is the center of our desires. He defines our self-worth not the status of being in a relationship.

Friendship. We had spent a little more than two years getting to know each other. This meant countless hours having fun together and asking each other hard questions. True intimacy grows slowly out of the solid soil of "knowing" each other casually and intently.

Support. We kept our relationship within sight of our families. One of the first steps Michael took was to ask my dad for permission to marry me, as well as for his blessing on our life together.

Purity. Nothing can ruin a relationship quicker than going too far, too fast, too soon. We're proud we made a commitment to stay sexually pure for each other—and for God.

As Michael and I stood there on the ridge, soaking in the beauty of our surroundings, he reached into his jacket pocket and pulled out a small velvet box. He handed it to me and smiled. "I have an early Christmas gift for you," he said.

I ran my finger across the lid and smiled back. "I bet it's jewelry!"

As he reached over and gently pulled out a diamond engagement ring, the expression on my face gave away my answer to the question he was about to ask. (As if he didn't already know!)

He knelt. "I couldn't imagine spending the rest of this life without you," Michael said, looking into my eyes. "Will you marry me?"

My smile grew even bigger. "*Yes!*"

Before we headed down the mountain to share the news with my family, Michael bowed his head and began talking to our heavenly Father: "Thank You, God, for bringing us together," he prayed out loud. "Waiting for each other has been worth it. We give You this marriage. Bless it, and let Your will be done in our life together."

• • •

To pursue a life of purity and holiness—to be set apart for God and learn how to be more like Jesus—we need to have control over our bodies and our minds. If our bodies are temples for the Holy Spirit, we need to make sure they're a place fit for God to dwell.

Here's how popular author and Christian scholar Jerry Bridges describes holiness: "This is a topic that has the possibility of sounding legalistic. But that's not what this is about at all. It's about balance. This concept can help us keep some control over the things that may become idols for us—food, alcohol, drugs—and the things that can lead us away from the [pursuit of holiness]—lustful thoughts, hatred, gossip."[9]

Purity goes hand in hand with holiness. It's not about being good enough, and it's much more than staying clear of an invisible "sin line." It's a whole mind-set. It's a heart issue. Do we want what God wants? Do we want to do things His way? Do we desire His standards?

Question: "Why all the rules regarding a person's sexuality? Why label certain activities as *sinful?*"

Sex is great in the right setting—marriage. We label sex as sinful if it happens outside of holy matrimony because that's what the Bible calls it. See Exodus 20:14; Matthew 5:27–30; 1 Corinthians 6:15–20, 7:2, 9; and 1 Thessalonians 4:3–8.

Question: "If two unmarried people agree to have sex, what's the big deal?"

Sex is a big deal. There's a lot of responsibility that comes with an intimate physical relationship: to God, the guy, your family, his family, his future wife, your future husband, yourself. Sex is much more than adult recreation. For married couples, intercourse creates a deep, powerful bond—sort of a relational superglue. And that bond is intended to be shared for a lifetime.

Question: "What if I've already blown it sexually? Can I regain my purity?"

Absolutely. Begin by working through the shame—what the devil uses to convince you that, because of your past, you are bad, worthless, beyond God's forgiveness. Regardless of what you've done, how many times, or with whom, there's hope and forgiveness in Jesus. He wants you to experience both. He wants to restore your purity. Don't waste another moment. Go to Him in prayer.

A FAITH THAT BREATHES

. . .has a passion for sexual purity. It breaks God's heart when He sees how casually sex is treated in our society, but it makes Him especially proud when He sees His followers living right—remaining pure and respecting the opposite sex. Right now as a Christian young lady, make a purity covenant with God. Even if you've already blown it sexually, ask God to help you remain pure from this point on.

. . .hungers for holiness. If we have asked the Holy Spirit to live in our hearts, we will show it through a life of purity and holiness. Do you have the fruit of the Spirit (Galatians 5:22–23)? Do you walk by the Spirit and have you crucified the sinful nature (Galatians 5:24–25)?

. . .is intolerant of immorality. God is not impressed with how long we can endure temptation but by how fast we can run from

it. Too often, we tease ourselves: walking up to the line with a date, buying the latest low-cut fashions, reading racy romance novels, watching movies that aren't worth our time or money. The Bible tells us not to allow even a *hint* of impurity in our lives.

JACI VELASQUEZ

It's Time for Some Pure Excitement

Consider this: Deciding to stay pure and keeping that promise are two different things. When we're in love with someone, there are times when keeping that promise is not easy. When a guy and girl kiss, it can easily get passionate. That's why we need to set our standards ahead of time and have an internal alarm that screams, "*Stop!*" Then communicate this to your boyfriend: "Don't touch me in that way. I don't want to feel like that. Because if I feel that, I'm going to want more. And I don't want to get out of control."

When you kiss, you love that, and it's really good. But it's never enough. You want something else. It's natural to want it, of course, but God has reserved that blessing for those who commit themselves to each other for life in marriage.

I know it's easy to get into situations that are very difficult to get out of. And I know that it's easy for girls to blame guys for putting the pressure on to have sex. Let's face it, it would be great if a guy would take the leadership role and use self-control to stop things before they begin to get out of hand. It's important for both guys and girls to commit themselves to abstinence and to set clear physical limits.

What it really comes down to is being responsible for yourself—for your own body and your own choices. You can't blame anyone else for a sexual situation that goes out of control—unless you're talking about rape.

Now the really hard question, the one I get asked occasionally in letters: What if you've already given yourself away and feel horrible about it? Will it ever be the same again?

The answer is yes. . .and no. You can't be a virgin again,

but you can be a virgin in your heart again. God can restore your innocence if you ask Him to, and the Holy Spirit will keep you in line if you ask Him to help you keep your promise.

mixed signals: guy/girl communication differences

> He who conceals his hatred has lying lips, and whoever
> spreads slander is a fool. When words are many, sin is not
> absent, but he who holds his tongue is wise. The tongue of
> the righteous is choice silver, but the heart of the wicked is
> of little value. The lips of the righteous nourish many, but
> fools die for lack of judgment.
>
> —PROVERBS 10:18–21

All evening, Jim had troubles communicating with Diane. Now he'd reached his breaking point. *What is with her? What does she want from me?*

The restaurant where they had come to dine was filled with the usual buzz of conversation, clinking silverware, and mouthwatering aromas. But Jim and Diane sat at opposite ends of the table, Diane toying with her chicken salad and Jim munching his barbecued ribs as he replayed the evening in his mind.

I picked her up at her house and whisked her off to what I was sure would be a knockout evening at our favorite dinner spot. In the car, I told her all about my day and she—well, she didn't say a word. Then, when I opened the door to the restaurant and commented about how I love coming here with her, that's when she lobbed a stinging comment: "Are you sure you mean me—or one of your past girlfriends?"

Jim took a sip of water, then cleared his throat. *Got to defuse this bomb.* "Uh, look, hon—out the window. Isn't that the most beautiful blue sky you've ever seen?"

"It's okay. But clouds are rolling in. It'll rain soon. It always does."

Okay, new approach. "Uh, are you having a bad day or something?"

Diane just glared at him.

Jim leaned back in his chair. "Please, talk to me. What's wrong? Why are you acting this way?"

That's when she let him have it. "A few days ago, you called me. 'Hello, Diane,' you said. 'How'd you like to go out?'"

" 'Sure,' " I responded.

" 'Great,' " you said. " 'I'll think up some place fun to go, then call you with the details.' "

"I was thrilled, but you never called back. . .until, let's see, two hours ago. Then you said you'd pick me up around seven and didn't show up until almost eight. And so I just sat there, feeling very foolish, wondering if you would even come at all. Then my mind began to play games with me: *What if he got in an accident? Is he okay?*

a woman of purity— 167

Maybe he isn't interested in me anymore. Maybe he's out with someone else. Does he think the world revolves around him. . .and that I'm supposed to just wait here by the phone? What an insensitive jerk!"

Diane moved forward and locked eyes with Jim. "If you really care about me, then show some respect. Above all. . .*communicate* with me!"

Jim just sat at the table with his mouth wide open—and, as usual, unsure about how to connect.

• • •

Sound familiar? Does this scenario describe some of your conversations with members of the opposite sex? At times we all feel that the entire male population is deaf to the sound of our voices. "I get no response," we tell ourselves. "I speak up and end up feeling that I am talking to myself. Am I going mad?"

And most of us have experienced the emptiness that comes from feeling tuned out. Listening is an act of love—or, at a more basic level, an act of simple consideration.

All communication requires two basic things: a speaking voice and a listening ear. This sounds pretty simple, but it's not. Most of us are very selective listeners, tuning in and tuning out as our interests dictate. With all the extraneous noise and worthless static that bombards us daily, this skill can be a blessing. It is something else, however, when we find ourselves tuning out those we say we love.

Yet this is exactly how Diane felt: tuned out. And

it hurt deeply because it came from the man she was trying to connect with.

Through the months, Diane had invested her heart into this relationship—grounding it in friendship, faith, and purity. Though Jim was a godly man, it was important for the two of them to work through some communication "static." Their future together depended upon it. A few days after expressing her frustration, she took one more step—writing a note that detailed her deepest "connection needs."

> Jim, I need you to. . .
> . . .choke back the temptation to supply all the answers.
> . . .take me seriously.
> . . .not be uncomfortable with moments of silence.
> . . .listen for more than just words. Listen to the feelings behind the words.
> . . .affirm me for who I am and for who I am becoming.
> . . .take my side at times.
> . . .listen to me —with your ears and your heart.

A FAITH THAT BREATHES

. . . is clued into male/female communication differences. For guys, a conversation is often a way to define a problem, debate the rights and wrongs, and find a solution. But most women would rather have a friendly ear from a man instead of advice. We often view conversation as a way of sharing our emotions with the listener. We talk until we feel better. Understanding communication styles and differences will enable you to connect better with the men in your life.

. . .connects with encouraging words. Mark Twain once said he could go for two months on a good compliment. Likewise, every one of us needs to be appreciated—to be applauded—for the awesome and unique person God made us. We need others to recognize our strengths or sometimes just to prop us up in the places where we tend to lean a little. Honest compliments are simple and cost nothing to give, but we must not underestimate their worth. (Follow Diane's lead: Consider sharing this need with the opposite sex.)

OUT OF EDEN
How to Date and Relate!

They're a hot R&B/pop trio—Lisa Kimmey and her sisters, Danielle and Andrea Kimmey Baca, were discovered by Toby McKeehan of dc Talk nearly a decade ago. Since then, they've cut several hit albums on Toby's record label (Gotee) and have set a high standard for Christian music.

Lisa explains. "I was working at a pizza place in the mall," she says, "and Toby walked in, told me that he had seen us perform, and asked me if we'd like to sign with Gotee. We didn't have to think very long! We were the first artists on his label."

Here are their thoughts on dating, relating, and the whole guy/girl communication thing.

Danielle on "Communication Starters"
When you talk to guys, cut the game-playing, "I've-got-to-be-cool" act. It's best when two people can relax, be real, and reveal who they are on the inside. Ladies, this is one area where you can take the lead: conversation. Do your best to set a relaxed tone. What kinds of things should you talk about? Anything—the day, an incident that happened, or your feelings and emotions. Above all, don't try to only say things you think guys want to hear.

Andrea on "Communicating Your Interest in a Guy"
Although I'm old-fashioned and think that guys should make the first move, it's okay for a woman to kick-start a potential relationship. Be honest and say something like, "I really think

I'm interested in you, and I think there's something there," or "I really admire you." Compliment him. Also, let him know how you feel through nonverbal communication: smiles, listening intently, spending time with him. If you start sensing that he's not interested, then move on. Above all, don't eat yourself up wondering if he likes you or not.

Lisa on "The 'Perfect Body' Pressure"

Aren't you tired of the pressure? You know, that unrealistic expectation to look like Britney Spears or the latest supermodel. It shouldn't surprise us that there are so many cases of anorexia or bulimia and girls trying to fit into unrealistic body images. And the two main sources of this pressure are glamour mags and guys, right? It seems as if every other magazine feeds the "perfect body" lie. What's more, the men in our lives are constantly bombarded with completely unrealistic images of what real women look like. And they pass those expectations on to us. It's time to begin thinking differently about beauty. The Word of God says that a woman should be of character and be honored by her character.

from rejection to connection

"I will not leave you as orphans; I will come to you."

—JOHN 14:18

Someone once wrote, "There is no use waiting for your love boat unless you've sent it out." Whether you're searching for a life mate, a dating relationship, or just one good friend to lean on, there's wisdom packed into these simple words. In fact, this advice was beautifully illustrated in a college classroom a few years back.

Dr. Leo Buscaglia was a professor at the University of Nevada. He taught what was called the "Love Class." Although we're unsure whether Buscaglia professed a faith in God, he wrote several books on love—more than a dozen to be exact—and had many positive insights on relationships. In his book *Born for Love*, he told of a lesson his students would never forget:

> When I was teaching Love Class, we were once visited by a dog. The dog entered the class fearlessly, wagging its tail and wandering among the seated students, getting all the attention he wanted. The students, of course, responded with

pats and caresses, prompting one of the young ladies in the class to observe dryly, "This is so typical of my life. Here I've been hurting all evening with loneliness and not a person has offered me an understanding touch. A stray dog wanders in and is showered with affection! There's something very wrong with that."

"Maybe it's not so crazy," a young man responded. "The dog came in and by his actions told us he was open to loving. His message was simple, nonthreatening, and clear. You, on the other hand, just sat there stoically, revealing nothing. We're not mind readers. Sometimes you've just got to speak up or at least give some hints." [10]

• • •

Want more friends? Searching for a meaningful relationship—perhaps even a marriage partner? Visibility is the key. Sitting quietly in the corner, "revealing nothing," just doesn't cut it.

Yet it's as if some women are locked in a cell of loneliness, often paralyzed by the fear of rejection. Too many of us have been programmed since childhood to avoid this trauma. But when you think about it, this shouldn't come as a surprise—just take a look at Webster's definition of the word *rejection:* "To discard or throw out as worthless, useless or substandard; to rebuff, deny acceptance, care and love to someone."

All relationships involve risk. Each time we connect with another person, we're making ourselves vulnerable—

putting our heart and emotions on the line. Like it or not, any "human connection" may involve some degree of rejection.

So, as we enter the social scene and make ourselves available to loving others and to being loved, how can we guard our hearts? Although there isn't a can't-lose formula that will solve every dilemma, here are some practical insights to consider:

Insights for friendship connections: From the start of a relationship, commit Isaiah 22:22 to prayer and apply it to your circumstances: "I will place on his shoulder the key to the house of David; what he opens no one can shut, and what he shuts no one can open." Ask God for wisdom every step of the way, during fun moments and the tough times. And trust that He has your best interests in mind.

Insights for dating connections: One of the most hurtful things anyone can do in a relationship is to play head games with a date. Leading someone to believe you have deeper feelings than you do can be devastating. And most of us are such pros at playing games that many times we don't even realize we're doing it. For instance, writing "I love you" notes just because it feels good at the time (perhaps you're in an especially good mood) and calling constantly communicate one thing: "I'm crazy about you and I'm committed to you." But if your heart doesn't match your actions, you're playing a brutal game.

Insights for all connections: Whether you're in a dating relationship or are nurturing a deep friendship, learn the art of good conversation skills. Ask questions of others that will go beyond yes/no answers. This enables you to learn more about him on the inside and lets him know you care. Too often, we'll meet someone who's such a good listener that he'll gladly do all the receiving—listening to us for hours—and we end up neglecting him (and not really getting to know much about him).

Here's one last idea for moving from rejection to connection on the dating scene. Pam, a twenty-something businesswoman in Nashville, found success through her pool of friends. Take a look at her story:

> *Friends are a big help. My relationship with the guy I'm dating now all came about in a weird way. Basically, he saw my picture on a poster at church. (I was speaking at an upcoming retreat.) He approached one of the pastors—a very close friend of mine—and asked, "Who is this lady?"*
>
> *The pastor responded, "Oh, you guys have to meet!"*
>
> *The whole matchmaker thing happened. The pastor filled me in about this guy. . .and I ended up taking his advice. If my friend recommended this guy, then I knew he must be pretty solid. We talked on the phone for three months*

*before we ever met each other. And when we
started dating, wow, I was happy I had been
introduced to him.*

*I suggest you tap into your circle of friends.
They can be the best help in finding the right
person to date—and perhaps lessen the blow of
rejection later. Why? If your friendship is close at
all, then they know you, as well as the kind of
person you'd be interested in. They can also help
you avoid getting into a miserable situation.*

A FAITH THAT BREATHES

. . .knows how love is supposed to be expressed:
"Love is patient, love is kind. It does not
envy, it does not boast, it is not proud. It is
not rude, it is not self-seeking, it is not easily
angered, it keeps no record of wrongs. Love
does not delight in evil but rejoices with the
truth. It always protects, always trusts, always
hopes, always perseveres. Love never fails" (1
Corinthians 13:4–8).

. . .is secure about what God thinks of us. Why?
Because God is secure in who He is. Therefore, He loves us unconditionally and without
giving a second thought to our flaws and
shortcomings—or how many times we've
been rejected. And that's how He wants us to
treat others. When we love others unconditionally—forgiving them and reaching out to

them—we are actually modeling God's love.

. . .*connects daily with Christ.* Pray. Pour out your heart and tell Jesus everything you're feeling—especially when it comes to relationships and rejection. *I feel alone. . .angry. . .jealous. . . scared. . .* Don't worry, nothing you say will shock the Lord or cause Him to love you any less. He's felt the same things, too, you know.

SARAH KELLY
"Take Me Away"

Those three little words—"Take Me Away"—make up the title cut on my first album with Gotee. But they also represent the journey I've been on for the last few years. There have been times when I've argued with God and hid in a corner, saying, "No, not me! You want someone else who's much better than me."

We all do this, don't we? It's usually an issue of self-esteem. We fear failure—and we fear rejection. It's easier to just hide in a corner than to take a risk. We do this with other people, especially when it comes to relationships.

Yet God wants us to make connections—with Him and with others. He wants us to live boldly and confidently, trusting Him in all circumstances.

The rest of the song I wrote is about me finally giving in to God's will—making a connection—by saying, "If this is really what You want from me, then take me away, because all that I love is You. Never have I felt so alone, but my, how I've grown."

We all go through tough situations in life. For some, it's divorce, for others, it's another kind of loss—a miscarriage, a broken relationship, a missed opportunity. Sometimes it's the turmoil that a teenager feels when she doesn't feel as if she fits in. We all have those moments when we think, *If there's a God, He must be a cruel jokester.*

But it's in the middle of those moments that we need to connect with God and chose to trust Him despite our senseless situations.

I can't help noticing that people tend to use worship as an escape by leaving their problems at the door—coming in to worship—and then picking up their problems when they leave. What we should be doing is entering into God's presence with our problems, doubts, and frustrations. We must be honest. We are free to worship God in the midst of our circumstances.

When I finally made this connection, it changed my life.

friendship foundations

"My command is this: Love each other as I have loved you.

Greater love has no one than this,

that he lay down his life for his friends.

You are my friends if you do what I command.

I no longer call you servants,

because a servant does not know his master's business.

Instead, I have called you friends, for everything that I

learned from my Father I have made known to you."

—JOHN 15:12–15

Take note of what Jesus said in the passage above: " 'I no longer call you servants. . . . I have called you friends.' "

All of us are defined by our roster of friends, and to have Jesus at the top of the list makes the best statement of identity.[11] You may be a follower of Christ, but do you approach Him as a friend?

Through the ages, our Lord and Savior has never stopped pursuing the friendship of human beings:

- Luther was so overwhelmed that he cried out his friendship in defense of the very studies of his liturgical, traditional faith.
- Pascal agreed that this friendship was the

answer to his longing, that there is a God-shaped vacuum at the heart of all of us. Only God can fill that vacuum.

- C. S. Lewis felt this pursuing love and claimed he was "surprised by joy."

Many of the world's most notable Christians have felt the chase of this pursuing lover. Jesus follows after us until at last He catches our hearts and the relationship is firm.[12] Author Harry Emerson Fosdick takes us back to the days Christ walked among us and reveals a tender "snapshot" of our Lord's friendship with His female disciples:

> The prominence of women among Jesus' first devoted and loyal contemporaries is notable. They were drawn to Him alike by their needs and by His masterful personality and message. They came for healing, for forgiveness, for power to lead a new life, and for His benediction on their children. The timid woman who touched the hem of His garment, and when found out "came in fear and trembling" to thank Him; the aggressive Canaanite woman, who would not be put off by the fact that she was not of Jewish race or faith; the women who provided for Him out of their means; and the mothers whose children He took "in his arms and blessed. . .laying his hands upon them," are typical.
>
> There is no explaining how that first

precarious movement of thought and life that Jesus started, with so much against it, and humanly speaking, so little for it, moved out into its world-transforming influence, without taking into account the response of womanhood to Jesus.

When they were sunk in sin, He forgave them; when they were humiliated, He stood up for them; when they suffered social wrongs, He defended them; when they had abilities to offer, He used them; and when they became sentimental and effusive in their devotion to Him, He stopped them: "A woman in the crowd raised her voice and said to him, 'Blessed is the womb that bore you, and the breasts that you sucked!' But he said, 'Blessed rather are those who hear the word of God and keep it.'"

• • •

Friendship Makers: Nothing strengthens a friendship more than two people sharing their thoughts and feelings with each other. God has given us the gift of communication. By using that gift, we come to know one another, to understand one another, and to love one another. Two souls become one through mutual sharing.

Friendship Breakers: At the same time, nothing ruins a friendship more quickly than betraying a confidence through gossip. Not only do secrets passed on become common property, but they usually grow as the story is told from one person to another. In the end, there are no winners, only losers.

Do you have an irresistible urge to tell secrets? Count the cost first.

Friendship According to God: God wants our hearts. He wants us to make friendship with Jesus our No. 1 priority—which means obeying His commands and loving others as He has loved us. (See John 15:9–17 for a more detailed explanation.)

In Matthew 22:37–39, Jesus tells us, " 'Love the Lord your God with all your heart and with all your soul and with all your mind.' This is the first and greatest commandment. And the second is like it: 'Love your neighbor as yourself.' "

A FAITH THAT BREATHES

. . .follows Christ's example by seeking out friends.

- *Reach out.* Take the first step and connect with someone.

- *Love the lonely.* Look around you. It's not hard to find someone who desperately needs a friend—especially those the world tries to ignore.

- *Give a smile.* Friendliness puts people at ease and lets them open up.

- *Don't fear rejection.* Not everyone will like you. Don't take it personally; perhaps your personalities just didn't click. You're fortunate if you have two or three really true buddies.

KRISTIN SWINFORD
(ZOEgirl)
Wanted—Real Friends

Friends are important to me, and I'm fortunate to have some solid friendship foundations.

A lady I know from Belmont University, named Dawn, is a good example. She and I are true kindred spirits. We can be totally real with each other about anything. And even though we live miles apart today, she'll call me out of the blue and will ask how I'm doing. Then she'll offer to pray with me. She encourages and blesses me and plays a big part in shaping my life—especially in helping me to stay on track with God.

Another friend is a woman named Shannon. I value her opinion. We have grown up together and have watched each other move through the different stages of life. I can always count on Shannon to give her honest opinion on tough topics. So when I'm confronted with a big decision, it's easier to consider another perspective when it comes from a loving and honest friend.

My band mates—Chrissy Conway and Alisa Girard—are amazing friends. God has given us a lot of grace, and we care deeply about each other. Yet there are those times when I'm tired, when we've been on the road for months—and I really just want to find some time for myself. I'm thankful that Chrissy and Alisa are sensitive to this and that we each strive to give each other plenty of privacy and personal space. Though we love to hang out and confide in one another, we make an effort to have friendships outside the group. Though we're one group, we're still three different personalities.

Each of these examples I've shared reveals a different

quality of true friendship: a kindred spirit (someone you can be real with), a great listener, and someone who shows you respect.

True friends help me to feel comfortable. True friends are understanding—people I connect with heart to heart. They are the ones who are looking out for me—while I'm looking out for them. Above all, genuine friends can vault us to new heights—and help us through unwanted lows.

A true friend. . .

    . . .tunes in to what I have to say.

    . . .allows me to be myself.

    . . .is honest at all times.

    . . .builds me up.

    . . .cares about my well-being.

    . . .looks out for my best interests.

altering God's plan?

These are rebellious people, deceitful children,

children unwilling to listen to the LORD's instruction.

—ISAIAH 30:9

Lights flashed, the television cameras zoomed in, and out walked queen of TV talk shows—Oprah Winfrey. Today's topic: homosexuality.

As the audience thundered with applause, seventeen-year-old Melissa Wagner swallowed hard—wondering what she'd gotten herself into.

Tell me what to say, God, the Chicago-area teen prayed silently. *This is not my soapbox. But there must be a reason I'm here today, and if You can use me, I'm available.*

Minutes before the show began, Melissa had been picked out of the audience to share her Christian perspective on homosexuality.

"Oprah professes to be a devout Christian," the producer had told the audience earlier. "Yet she does not believe that it's wrong if a person chooses to be gay. Anyone here have a problem with that?"

Melissa couldn't keep quiet. *How can Oprah profess to be a devout Christian yet not follow what God's Word says about homosexuality? I've got to speak up!*

She stood up and raised her hand. Then the words shot out of her mouth: "Yeah, I'm a Christian. . .and I have a problem with that."

"Would you be willing to say that on national TV?" the producer asked.

"Yeah. . .I, uh. . .guess so."

Now the moment had arrived, and all eyes were on Melissa.

"I think you're a powerful woman," Melissa told Oprah on live TV. "Lots of people look up to you. But if you label yourself a Christian and also say you support the homosexual lifestyle, you're contradicting yourself."

Oprah told Melissa that she only believes *parts* of the Bible—not the entire book. "The God I serve doesn't care if you're tall, short, black, white, fat, skinny, gay, or lesbian," Oprah said. "He loves everybody."

Melissa tried to speak up again, but Oprah cut her off—and turned to members of the audience who supported homosexuality. Melissa wanted to say that God *does* love everyone—that's what His death on the cross was all about. She wanted to say that He loves *all* sinners! He *doesn't,* however, love the sin that's corrupting our lives.

"Where do you draw the line, Oprah?" Melissa finally was able to ask. "How can you decide what you will and won't accept as truth from the Bible? A Christian is one who is a devoted follower of Jesus Christ and *all* He stands for."

Oprah had her comeback ready. "My definition of Christianity is different than yours," she fired back. She told how she believed that Allah and Buddha and several other paths lead to heaven.

"I believe what John 14:6 says," Melissa said. " ' "I am the way and the truth and the life. No one comes to the Father except through me." ' That's so clear. It eliminates all false teaching."

Toward the end of the show, Melissa was crying. The camera zoomed in on her standing at the mike with tears streaming down her face.[13]

• • •

Several months after the *Oprah* taping had aired, here's how Melissa summed up her experience: "It probably sounded like one more wimpy Christian who was unable to articulate her beliefs. But the truth is, I wasn't crying because Oprah was on my case—though she continually badgered me throughout the entire show. I was crying because she simply doesn't get it. The studio audience didn't get it. Our culture doesn't get it. We're being deceived and fed a pack of lies from the father of lies himself."

When it comes to hotly debated issues such as homosexuality, do you get it—what the Bible says, that is? Or are you being pulled into "cultural Christianity"—what's popular at the moment—instead of the unchanging, absolute truth of God?

It's little wonder that some Christians are confused, considering the sexual climate we live in. For example, gay clubs are a part of many college campuses. Even gay high school proms are springing up around the country. In New Orleans, organizers utilized a funeral home for the multi-school function. Near Chicago, the First Congregational United Church of Christ in Naperville hosted a mixer for suburban students. (The event was sponsored by the Gay-Straight Alliance at Wheaton Warrenville South High School.)

"This is more than symbolic. This is a big step," Nancy Mullen, executive director of DuPage Questioning Youth Center, said in an interview with the *Chicago Tribune*. "Every other kid gets to go to a prom as they so choose, but for [gay students] that's not an option."

Yet there are many who, like Melissa, take seriously the Lord's instruction—even if they are politically incorrect. Take the thousands of young people who marched in the national capitals of Canada and the United States a few years back. Proud of their virginity—and not afraid to admit it—many signed "True Love Waits" cards, proclaiming: "We are committed to Christ."

More than 210,000 of these cards were displayed in Washington, D.C., and Ottawa as a visual representation of young singles who have a passion for purity.

A moral revolution is emerging from the darkness. Are you a part of it?

A FAITH THAT BREATHES

. . .understands that struggling with same-sex attraction isn't a sin, but acting upon these desires is.

Prayer is one really important defense in this battle. It's also important to realize that these kinds of feelings may not go away overnight. Opening up doors in our thought lives or through our actions with others could potentially fuel our confusion, as well as the depth of our struggle.

. . . *knows that "gay" does not describe who a person is.* Instead, it's a political term that describes a chosen identity or lifestyle. Despite the arguments we may have heard, men and women simply are not born homosexual. God did not design us this way.

. . . *turns to Christ with every sexual struggle.* Even during those moments when Satan tries to trip us up, Jesus loves us and cares deeply about our battles. (He understands them better than we do.) He can help us overcome anything. We must tell Him everything we're feeling and ask Him for guidance. We can pray anytime, anywhere. Jesus forgives and heals and delivers.

. . . *is tuned into God's instructions about sexuality:* "Flee from sexual immorality. All other sins a man commits are outside his body, but he who sins sexually sins against his own body. Do you not know that your body is a temple of the

Holy Spirit, who is in you, whom you have received from God? You are not your own; you were bought at a price. Therefore honor God with your body" (1 Corinthians 6:18–20).

"Do not be deceived: Neither the sexually immoral nor idolaters nor adulterers nor male prostitutes nor homosexual offenders nor thieves nor the greedy nor drunkards nor slanderers nor swindlers will inherit the kingdom of God" (1 Corinthians 6:9–10).

"They exchanged the truth of God for a lie. . . . Men also abandoned natural relations with women and were inflamed with lust for one another. Men committed indecent acts with other men, and received in themselves the due penalty for their perversion" (Romans 1:25, 27).

RACHAEL LAMPA
A Passion for God's Plan

Her pop sound tops the charts and her message about God captivates the heart. Here are Rachael Lampa's thoughts on purity, faith, and family.

Purity

I completely believe that God created sex to be shared as a lifelong bond between a husband and wife. It's designed for the creation of a family. It diminishes its purpose when it is used wrongly and disrespectfully. Sex is God's creation—a beautiful creation. Yet when it's used wrongly, its beauty is diminished. Here's how I view my own sexuality: My body is a temple for the Holy Spirit. (See 1 Corinthians for some wonderful passages on this topic.) I remind myself daily that I am a temple for the Lord. This truth guides my choices.

Attractive Qualities

My faith and belief in God are the qualities I'm most proud of. And when it comes to close relationships, I try to connect with others who possess these qualities, too. I try to surround myself with people who I know will help me grow, as well as encourage and challenge me. And when it comes to the dating scene, I'm only going to commit my time to a guy who is reaching for the same goals. I admire guys who have a passion for the Lord. Above all, I get to know someone before dating him. I guard my heart. We are all so different and operate in so many ways that we all have to find the right way to date.

Friendship

It's wonderful to be a light in other people's lives. But I'm very careful about how much time I spend with people who don't share my values. I know that I also need friends who are going to be supportive and help me grow stronger. I take a huge stand when it comes to living outside of the box. I try to live what I believe. I surround myself with the people I trust.

Spiritual Influences: My Family

My greatest spiritual influences in my life are my parents and my older brother. We are very close and do our best to keep God in the center of our lives. In fact, there have been moments when we've stopped what we were doing and began to pray together—especially when we were dealing with a conflict.

Through the years, I've discovered a key to having a strong relationship with your family: Humble yourself and say, "Okay, I may be wrong here. I want to see your perspective." It's godly and honorable to do this. Above all, we need to be ready to forgive others.

happy, whole—and single

> I wish that all men were as I am.
>
> But each man has his own gift from God;
>
> one has this gift, another has that.
>
> —1 CORINTHIANS 7:7

When you think about the gifts of the Holy Spirit, what kinds of things come to mind? Wisdom from the Lord? Serving others? Showing mercy? Teaching?

Consider yet another gift: singleness. That's right. The apostle Paul calls singleness a gift from God: "I wish that all men were as I am. But each man has his own gift from God; one has this gift, another has that" (1 Corinthians 7:7). Paul was determined to use this special gift as a way to serve and encourage other Christians. Because he did not have a wife, he knew he could devote himself wholeheartedly to his ministry.

C. S. Lewis, who spent most of his life as a bachelor, had an interesting perspective on the subject of singleness. In his book *Letters to an American Lady,* he says this about the issue of marriage versus singleness:

"I nominally have [a place of my own] and am nominally master of the house, but things seldom go as I would have chosen. The truth is that the only alternatives are either solitude (with all its miseries and dangers, both moral and physical) or else all the rubs and frustrations of a joint life. The second, even at its worst seems to me far the better. . . . We are *all* fallen creatures and *all* very hard to live with."[14]

Singleness can be good—the path God wants some to follow. It was for Paul—and, for that matter, it was right for Jesus. If this is what God wants for your life, then He'll make it a right and good experience. The Bible never talks about singleness as being second-rate. It need not be unfulfilled. It need not be unhappy.

Consider these observations from popular author Tim Stafford: "One of the saddest things I see is the tendency for single people to live life as though waiting for something or someone to happen to them. They act as though they are in limbo, waiting to become capable of life when the magic day at the altar comes. Of course, they're usually disappointed. In some cases they become such poor specimens of humanity that no one wants to marry them. More often they do get married only to discover that they haven't received the key to life: The initiative and character they should have developed before marriage is exactly what they need in marriage. And they are still left lonely and frustrated."[15]

As Stafford points out, one of the worst things you can do as a single person is to believe the lie that you are second-rate because you are not yet married. If God has truly given you the gift of singleness, be thankful and enjoy this gift to the fullest.

A FAITH THAT BREATHES

. . .isn't afraid to do some soul-searching. Why do I believe I should be married—or remain single? Could I handle the possibility of a lifetime of singleness? What are my real motives for pursuing dating relationships?

. . .nurtures a solid identity. It's important to have a grasp on who you are, whether you choose singleness or marriage.

. . .strives to be present-minded. Examine where you are in life. Look around and notice the beautiful day. Go out and play football or volleyball. Fill your time with joy.

. . .glances at a problem and gazes at God. If you feel lonely and discontent, focus on a solution, not the struggle. A wise Christian once noted: "Too many people gaze at a problem and glance at God. Instead, we must glance at our trials and fix our gaze on God. This is the key to uncovering a solution."

STACIE ORRICO
Single-Minded Pursuit

Is marriage in my future? I hope so. But right now, as a single woman, I'm living my life to its fullest, to be a whole person at this stage of my life. I want to make the most of what God has given me. My single-minded pursuit is knowing Jesus more deeply, more passionately—and striving to follow His plans for my life.

When it comes to my social life, there are three things I take very seriously:

Purity. I have a song on one of my records called "Everything." It's about abstinence and purity. Someday I'm going to give my husband everything. If you think about it, sex is the only thing that you can completely save for your husband. It is the one gift that I can give to him in perfect condition, and that thought makes it worth waiting for.

Godly dating. During my high school years, my family and I really believed in godly, group dating. I'd go out with groups of guys and girls—rather than one-on-one, romantic-type dating. The key was *fun!* In fact, we didn't even call it dating. Hanging out in groups was much more of a relaxed experience than traditional dating. The pressure was off, and I could be myself. There was always someone else to talk to or to sit with. In addition, I didn't have to hang out with the same person all evening.

Even though I'm now on my own, the core rules still apply: Guys I date must be godly, they must live their faith, and they must make purity a priority. Yet now my focus is on the future. Today, I ask myself different questions: Is this someone I could one day marry? Is he growing in Christ? Does this relationship honor God?

Sharing Christ. We usually don't mix this topic with the dating scene, but we should. I can't think of better conversations to have with guys—especially someone I'm considering having a relationship with—than my No. 1 relationship: Jesus.

People are called to share their faith in different ways, some through what they do—maybe their music—and some by sharing the gospel straight out. I think a lot of people need to trust somebody before they're gonna believe what he says. They need somebody who has taken the time to get to know them and show that they care, and that's why they want to share their faith.

the truth about marriage

> "I know the plans I have for you," declares the LORD,
>
> "plans to prosper you and not to harm you,
>
> plans to give you hope and a future."
>
> —JEREMIAH 29:11

One minute, we're surfing the TV—looking for something decent to watch—and the next minute, we're outraged. "What we're seeing can't be real!" I (Michael) tell Tiffany. "It's got to be staged. But why? Who actually lives this way?"

We've stumbled upon the *Ricki Lake Show*. Today's topic: "Transvestite Gay Men and Their Female Lovers." It's amazing what you encounter on daytime TV. (Remember the *Oprah* eye-opener on Day 26?)

Ricki Lake is interviewing a gay man named Charlie, who is dressed like a woman, and a lady named Sarah, who is dressed like a man. Both claim to be lovers. Suddenly, the woman pulls an engagement ring out of her jacket pocket and kneels in front of the man.

"Charlie, we've been friends for a long time," she says, "and you know how I feel about you."

The man blushes, and the audience starts cheering.

"I want to spend my life with you," Sarah tells Charlie, offering him the ring. "I want to have your children. That's why I'm asking you to marry me."

The audience roars even louder. Even Ricki begins to pressure him. "So, what's your answer, Charlie?" she says. "She obviously loves you. Are you going to say no to this beautiful lady?"

"But I'm gay," Charlie responds.

"I don't care," his lover says. "I think we can have a good life together."

After a long pause—the audience still cheering—Charlie looks at Ricki and says, "Yes—I'll marry her. But only because I love that gorgeous ring!"

• • •

As outrageous as this scenario may seem, it speaks of the casual attitudes our culture holds toward marriage. True, Charlie and Sarah represent an extreme case, certainly not the norm. Yet too many well-meaning couples—even Christian couples—move glibly through courtship and into marriage, not fully grasping just how much is at stake for them. And some of the reasons they give for heading down the aisle are just as weak as the one Charlie came up with:

> "All my friends and siblings have tied the knot."

> "I don't want to be alone."

> "I'm a romantic at heart who loves being in a relationship."

"My parents expect me to get married."

"Everybody at church will think I'm abnormal if I remain single."

When it comes to the matters of the heart, where do you stand? If marriage is in your future, and if you're currently in a relationship, how can you be certain that the romantic love you're experiencing today is the kind that will last tomorrow—and all the tomorrows to come? More specifically, at what point can you be confident that the man you're currently seeing is the person you should marry?

Next to committing your life to Jesus Christ, choosing a life mate is one of the biggest decisions you'll ever make—so you'd be wise to ponder these questions carefully and soberly. Above all, enter a romantic relationship with your eyes wide open, and bathe the whole experience in prayer. The fact is, a bad marriage is worse than not being married at all.

A FAITH THAT BREATHES

. . . *knows the secret to lifelong love.* If you're convinced that marriage is in your future, understand this: God doesn't expect you to search the earth for the *one-and-only* person He has in mind for you. (What are the chances of ever finding that person?) Instead, He gives us a promise. (Go back and reread it in Jeremiah 29:11.) When it comes to relationships, the

Lord is instructing us to walk by faith. He also
wants us to use our head and ask some tough
questions (see discussion below), understand
what lasting love is all about, and avoid being
"unequally yoked."

. . . *isn't afraid to ask some tough questions:* What
qualities are important in the man or woman
I marry? Does he love Jesus? Does he share
some of my dreams and life goals? Do I enjoy
his company?

. . . *understands what lasting love is all about.*
In the Bible, the word *love* often refers
to action—something we *do* rather than
something we *feel*. John 3:16 says, " 'God so
loved the world that he gave. . .' " This verse
refers to love as an action—something that
God did for us. In other places throughout
Scripture, love is defined as selfless giving
to others; manifesting attitudes of kindness,
patience, and humility; and commitment
in relationships. So, what does love as an
action have to do with the warm, fuzzy, head-
over-heels kind we experience in romantic
relationships? Everything. The kind of love
we share with a marriage partner goes way
beyond simple emotions. This kind of love
involves commitment. It means putting the
needs of another above your own: "It is not

rude, it is not self-seeking, it is not easily angered, it keeps no record of wrongs. Love does not delight in evil but rejoices with the truth" (1 Corinthians 13:5–6).

. . .avoids being "unequally yoked." Let's go straight to the Bible for some direction regarding this issue. Take a look at 2 Corinthians 6:14–15. It says, "Do not be yoked together with unbelievers. For what do righteousness and wickedness have in common? Or what fellowship can light have with darkness? . . . What does a believer have in common with an unbeliever?" These are good questions to ask yourself. The fact is, when two people are yoked together, they must both pull in the same direction. By definition, Christians and non-Christians are headed in different directions. Become unequally yoked in a romantic relationship, and you've got disaster. (The couple ends up going nowhere, and they keep rubbing sores on each other in the process.) Getting involved romantically with a non-Christian just won't work. It's best to find a mate who is committed to living a godly life.

NATALIE GRANT

How I Met My Husband

I got my first recording deal and needed to do a concert for the record company. I had just moved to Nashville and didn't know any musicians, so the A&R rep recommended two piano players. She suggested a guy named Byron and one named Bernie. I called Byron because his was the first number I had. He couldn't do it. Then I called Bernie, who's a really close friend of Byron's.

We ended up connecting and doing a concert together. I instantly called my family and said, "I met this guy I've dreamed about my whole life!"

Bernie had actually been engaged and was heartbroken at the time, so he was a lot more guarded than I was. We became really good friends for an entire year before we decided to go on our first date. Then we were married the next year!

I love married life. Being with my husband and spending time with my family in Seattle takes priority.

In fact, just hanging out at home is so important to me. I even love the mundane boring things in life—going to the grocery store, doing laundry, and sitting in our big, overstuffed brown chair. Our idea of a perfect night is being at home, watching a movie and having Chinese take-out!

a woman
of courage

driving out worldly fear

"But be sure to fear the LORD and serve him

faithfully with all your heart; consider what

great things he has done for you."

—1 SAMUEL 12:24

Fear. It's one of those words we don't like—unless we're at an amusement park.

When we're buckled into a roller coaster, we're pretty confident that nothing worse than losing our lunch is going to happen. And we're at least somewhat certain that the ride will be over in thirty seconds, gently delivering us back to that long line we waited in for thirty minutes—just to get scared!

"Amusement park fear" is acceptable because it's a mere imitation of real, raw, spine-tingling fear. It is actually entertaining.

On the other hand, the type of emotion most people connect with the word *fear* is terror: the fear of pain or damage to ourselves. Included in this definition is the fear of losing a friend, a loved one, or even our own lives. This type of fear can generate plenty of worry, stress, anxiety—can't it?

And every day, we experience low levels of "commonsense fear." You know, good, respect-inducing fear—the kind that tells us not to step into the street in front of an oncoming semi and to keep our fingers out of the flame. That little alarm triggers inside our heads, shouting: "Respect the consequences! Stay away from the things that can hurt or kill you!"

But let's explore yet another kind of fear. In several passages, the Bible tells us that (1) to fear God is the beginning of wisdom, (2) the fear of the Lord leads to life, and (3) the Lord delights in those who fear Him. What do you suppose it means by this style of fear? And why are there so many Scriptures that instruct us to fear God, not man?

• • •

The Lord wants to build in us the courage we need to walk boldly with Him. Charles H. Spurgeon explained it this way: "You will need the courage of a lion to pursue a course that could turn your best friend into your fiercest foe. For the sake of Jesus Christ, you must be courageous. Risking your reputation and emotions for the truth requires a degree of moral principle that only the Spirit of God can work into you. Do not turn back, do not be a coward; be a hero of the faith. Follow in your Master's steps. He walked this rough way before you."[16]

In order to give us courage and to develop strong character in us, God wants us to have a healthy fear of Him—the kind that is rooted in respect and reverence.

Our Savior also wants to drive out worldly fear—the sort that stems from doubt and condemnation—the type that leaves its victims panicked and paralyzed. . .and ineffective for service in God's kingdom.

To accomplish His goals, God wants us to take responsibility for our actions and to know that sin is serious business. (This is what is meant by "the fear of the LORD leads to life" [Proverbs 19:23].) One day we will all give account for our choices. This reality actually terrified Paul and motivated him to strive to please God in everything he did. (See 2 Corinthians 5:9–11.)

Christian author Henry Blackaby has also wrestled with this issue. In his book *Experiencing God,* here's what he concludes: "God does not force His will upon us. He will ask us to answer for the way we responded to Him. Christians have been pardoned by the sacrifice of Jesus. We are not condemned. But because God is absolutely just, we will be called on to give an account of our actions."[17]

In my walk with Christ, I (Vanessa) have sometimes found myself directly in harm's way. And during these moments, I've noticed three things going on inside me: I've feared for my own life, I've questioned whether I was ready to meet God, and I've felt the assurance of God's protection.

Call me crazy, but I think it's healthy to experience fear of this nature. It's good to assess the condition of our heart and, like Paul, strive to please God in everything we do. (Knowing that we'll give account for our actions is a healthy fear.) Above all, it's comforting to know that we are in the grip of His protection.

What's more, each time that I've faced the fear of man, the fear of God has overruled. And each time that I've gone up against the power of man, the power of God has overruled. *God is all-powerful and eternal.*

He protects us, nurtures our character, and drives out worldly fear.

A FAITH THAT BREATHES

... *knows that disobedience can result in devastating consequences.* Just look at King David's life. Even though he was completely forgiven for the sins of lust, adultery, robbery, and murder, God did not remove the consequences of his sin. (Read Psalm 103:12, as well as 2 Samuel 12–13.) What can we learn from this story? God wants us to have a serious reverence for His instructions. But when we blow it, He wants us to take responsibility for our actions by turning to Him in repentance. He will drive out the fear of doubt and condemnation and will give us the courage to follow His lead as we deal with the consequences.

... *is confident that a believer walks with the protection of our Lord Jesus Christ.* And even though He calls us to bear some burdens, some hurts, and some trials, He will continue to work in us, giving us a heart like His. This is our highest calling: living in respectful fear for the One who spoke the universe into being and who holds us in the palm of His loving hand.

. . .rejoices in the truth. He stepped down to save us and to bear the punishment for all our sins. He bought our freedom and gives complete forgiveness freely to anyone who asks. This powerful, almighty God is tender toward us and will never give us more than we can bear. He will always watch over us with a steady eye. He never blinks.

NICOLE C. MULLEN
Fear God, Not Man

I'm the great-great-great-great-granddaughter of a slave. In order for my family to endure, they had to be strong physically, spiritually, and mentally. So I come from good stock. I'm proud of that. But I'm even prouder that because I'm a Christian, my spiritual lineage now goes back to Abraham, Isaac, and Jacob.

I've been the brunt of racial slurs, and I've heard that some radio stations won't play my songs simply because of the color of my skin. There's still a need to promote racial unity in Christian circles. But at the same time, some people and stations have defied expectations by embracing me and my music.[18]

Even more important than my freedom as an African-American is the freedom that Christ has given me, because that is the only true liberty. (I've recorded a song about this, titled "Freedom.") This is why I get on stage and dance about it. I say, "I'm gonna get my 'shout' on!" The "shout" is something we're notorious for doing in charismatic and African-American churches. You do it with your feet—it's a dance of celebration.

With so much to celebrate, why fear man? Why fear the sin of this world? God has delivered me. I choose to trust Him.

lonely planet

One thing I ask of the LORD, this is what I seek:
that I may dwell in the house of the LORD all the days of my
life, to gaze upon the beauty of the LORD and to seek him in
his temple. For in the day of trouble he will keep me safe
in his dwelling; he will hide me in the shelter of his tabernacle and set me high upon a rock. Then my head will be
exalted above the enemies who surround me;
at his tabernacle will I sacrifice with shouts of joy;
I will sing and make music to the LORD.

—PSALM 27:4–6

Henri J. M. Nouwen—a Catholic priest whose incredible writing is so nutritious and filling—wrote these
powerful words:

> *There is much mental suffering in our world.
> But some of it is suffering for the wrong reason
> because it is born out of the false expectation
> that we are called to take each other's loneli-
> ness away. When our loneliness drives us away
> from ourselves into the arms of our companions
> in life, we are, in fact, driving ourselves into
> excruciating relationships, tiring friendships,*

*and suffocating embraces. . . . Friendship and
Love cannot develop in the form of an anxious
clinging to each other. They ask for gentle fear-
less space in which we can move to and from
each other.*[19]

Out of loneliness we find ourselves running into
the arms of another in order to satiate our intense
craving for companionship and our deep hunger for
validation. It is in the arms of another, we believe, that
we will find identity and definition—like one piece of
a great puzzle relying on another piece for wholeness
and purpose.

But we were not created for loneliness. God made
us for fellowship. And from the moment we come to
Him, He begins growing in us a garden fit for His habi-
tation. What is it like in your garden? Does the Lord
come to walk with you in the cool of the day? Do you
spend time walking arm in arm, hand in hand with
Him? Is there a time when He is your singular focus
and Source? Or, like Eve, have you chosen other fruit
to fulfill you? (Perhaps you've found yourself estranged
and exiled from His presence.)

• • •

If there is no investment in intimacy with God, then
the loneliness of exile only grows more and more overwhelming. We begin to feel that we, too, have been
cast out of His garden to toil to care for ourselves away
from His presence.

Outside His garden, our lives become defined by our environment and our fears. *Who will love me? Am I pretty enough? Who will want me now? How hard must I work to be accepted? Will this hard soil of my life ever bear the fruit of love and companionship?*

We become lonely, and after a while we begin to search desperately for that oasis in the desert that will refresh us and bring us life. Yet, in the arms of another, we can deceive ourselves and end up "drinking the sand." (The "cure" for our loneliness is sometimes merely an illusion.)

What's the difference, you might ask, between loneliness and solitude? Don't they both mean you are alone?

Yes, but *alone* and *lonely* are not the same things. Alone means you stand on your own two feet and sit with yourself in peace. Lonely means you run to and fro, looking for yourself reflected in the eyes of other people. It means you define yourself by the absence of companionship. This kind of loneliness keeps us constantly seeking the face of others for satisfaction.

Loneliness sometimes causes us to plaster ourselves against anyone who will dare get near enough to us. We open our hearts and our spirits and spill ourselves out upon the ground, desperate for the other person to soak us up and take us in.

How can you move from this kind of starving loneliness to a refreshing, fruitful solitude?

Solitude means sitting with God and seeking His heart for a reflection of your own. There is an alertness in solitude that tunes your senses to the incredible flow of life all around you. *Loneliness* means we expect someone else to supply the missing pieces in order for us to feel whole. We want them to plant themselves in our lives in order to help us bear the fruit of love.

Through solitude, we meet God in the deepest part of our heart and work together with Him to tend our garden. We put down deep roots in Him and allow Him to prune us so that the fruit of our lives will be plentiful.

In solitude, we find our identity through the creative initiative of Jesus. Solitude is having a quiet place with Him readily available at a moment's notice because it is just behind the door at which He is constantly knocking. He calls to us to come further in to the quiet and find ourselves there. In that space He defines us, He satisfies us, and He bears fruit in us. But we must turn off the television, turn away from the mall, power down our cell phones, and take the time to sit with Him.

So often we are running on empty and unwilling to search out the quiet stillness because we do not know how to sit and be ourselves. We are uneasy and fear the quiet. But this kind of existence is fruitless. Instead, we must come to the wellspring of life in the arms of Jesus.

As Rich Mullins once sang in "Calling Out Your Name," "I know this thirst will not last long, but it will soon drown in a song not sung in vain."

Don't sing your song in vain. Don't seek out the melody of others to refresh your spirit. Bring your starving loneliness to the Lord's table in the wilderness and find fulfillment and a fruitful solitude. Find yourself there.

. . .doesn't get bogged down by emotions. Take a moment to honestly evaluate your situation. Ask yourself some key questions:

- What is making me feel so lonely? Am I anxious about something? Is an unresolved issue at the root of my emotions?
- Am I comfortable in my own skin? Can't I find wholeness in the fact that I'm God's creation? Can't I still feel secure in my identity in Christ—even when I'm alone from time to time?
- What steps am I going to take to get through this loneliness?

. . .isn't afraid to get help. Seek the advice of your parents, pastor, or family physician. Sometimes you need to talk things out with people who are older and wiser. Above all, you need face-to-face interaction. Definitely get help if (1) you prefer isolation to the company of friends and family, or (2) feelings of loneliness and depression have persisted for several days in a row.

CHRISTINE DENTE

Stop the Loneliness Pattern

Growing up, I was a loner. And yet I had a million boyfriends, one after another, because I didn't want to feel alone—even though I often wanted to be alone. It was a very weird dichotomy—this very needy, lonely person who wanted to be alone and not be close with people yet who continually sought out emotional attachments with other people, mostly guys. And when I eventually met Scott, who is now my husband, it could have been just another emotional attachment for a while before I moved on. But the Lord decided that this was it. We're gonna stop the pattern![20]

Today, I'm happily married with a son and two daughters. It was God melting my lonely heart and helping me see myself through His eyes that changed my life.

Scott is the picture of Christ loving the church, giving Himself up for her. He pursued me through those thorns and those walls. He didn't give up, and he continues to be that way after more than sixteen years of marriage.

Jesus doesn't give up, either. He continues to fulfill His promise: "But we have this treasure in jars of clay to show that this all-surpassing power is from God and not from us. We are hard pressed on every side, but not crushed; perplexed, but not in despair; persecuted, but not abandoned; struck down, but not destroyed" (2 Corinthians 4:7–9).

when emotions get ugly

In you, O LORD, I have taken refuge;

let me never be put to shame.

Rescue me and deliver me in your righteousness;

turn your ear to me and save me.

Be my rock of refuge, to which I can always go;

give the command to save me, for you are my rock and my

fortress. Deliver me, O my God, from the hand of the

wicked, from the grasp of evil and cruel men.

—PSALM 71:1–4

I (Johanna) don't remember how old I was—maybe thirteen. But I remember the scene as if it happened yesterday. My parents had left me in charge of my younger siblings for the afternoon. (Some of you reading this can undoubtedly relate to this scenario.) On this particular afternoon—and in typical older-sister style—I was ordering my younger brother around like I was queen and he was my servant. But in typical pesky-little-brother style, he resisted.

That's when it happened. My anger started to simmer inside. Soon, it began to bubble and boil over. I found myself chasing him around the house, grabbing at his shirt, and screaming all the way. He ran upstairs and downstairs. He would try to shut doors between us to keep the livid she-devil (me) away. His fear manifested with a mix of crying and laughter, which only kindled my fire.

Finally, he ran out of the house—a good decision on his part. I didn't want any neighbors to see my ugly state, so I stayed hidden indoors. After locking the front door, I sat fuming in the kitchen. I had never been so angry in all my life. *Why won't he cooperate? I'm in charge; he should do what I say immediately—and without question!*

As I sat there, the scene played over and over in my mind. And as my screaming echoed back, I began to feel ashamed. How could I have done such a thing? I loved my brother, yet I treated him horribly.

It was as if some kind of wild banshee took over and I had lost touch with reality. At this moment, I felt deeply convicted of my sin. The thought of what my anger was capable of doing frightened me. I lowered my head and began to pray: "Lord, I'm so sorry. Please don't let this happen again."

• • •

Like most women, I can still get emotional—at least once a month. But I can honestly say that it has never reached the burning inferno that it did that afternoon years ago.

When I find my emotions heating up, I've learned to run straight to my Lord's throne room and tell Him all about my frustrations. In the midst of my complaining, He has a way of reminding me of how much He loves me and that He'll never stop working on me. He applies this salve to heal my hurt feelings, and He washes away my dirt and ugliness. In fact, He turns the ugliness into beauty.

Think of times when your worst has come out. Perhaps there is something in your life that is a constant battle to overcome. What if, when you looked into the mirror of God's Word, your ugliness was reflected back? You can't hide it or use some sort of makeup to cover it. Instead, try running straight into God's presence. He will always accept you no matter what you look like.

In the Gospel of Luke, we read about an encounter Jesus had with a sinful woman (Luke 7:36–50). The setting is a Pharisee's house at mealtime. The Pharisee was curious about Jesus and wanted to check Him out for himself. Just as they had situated themselves at the dinner table, a woman entered the room—a woman who was clearly not welcome in the Pharisee's house. It took a real boldness and a deep trust in Jesus for her to come in this way. She had a deep sense that Jesus would not send her away or be embarrassed to be seen with her. (I wonder if there is another story not included in scriptures of how Jesus won this woman's trust.)

Christ knew and the Pharisee knew that she had some serious sin issues in her life. Maybe she was a prostitute? Maybe she was a thief? Whatever the sin, she was ugly with it.

Somehow, she had found out that Jesus was a guest

at the Pharisee's house, and she seized her opportunity to confess her ugliness and sin to Jesus. In Christ's presence, she was overcome with conviction of her sins—so much so that she began to cry. She cried so many tears that they dripped all over Jesus' feet. From the Pharisee's point of view, she was a no-good, trespassing sinner with no regard for tradition and the rules of Jewish etiquette. He probably considered her emotional display to be an offensive charade.

But the woman didn't care about rules of etiquette, and neither did Jesus. She had something inside that needed to get out and be forgiven. She wanted to be made clean, and Jesus was the only One who could do it.

Simon, the Pharisee, mumbled to himself: "If Jesus really was a prophet, He would know who this woman is and what sins she has committed."

Simon was working on the assumption that if Jesus was a prophet, He would be offended by the woman's actions. True to form, however, Jesus replied to Simon's musings with a hypothetical question: "Simon, say that a creditor has two men owing him money. One guy owes five hundred bucks and the other fifty bucks. Neither of the men had the money to repay, yet the creditor graciously released them from their debts. Which man is going to like this creditor more?"

Simon replies, "I suppose the one for whom he canceled the larger debt."

"Correct," Jesus replied and then went further. "Simon, you didn't wash My feet with water when I arrived at your house, but this woman has washed My feet with her tears and dried them with her hair. You have not greeted Me with the traditional greeting of a kiss, and yet she hasn't stopped kissing My feet ever since I came in. You have not even anointed My head with oil, and here she has brought her most expensive perfumed oil to anoint My feet."

Jesus then forgave her sins because He saw that her heart was overflowing with love for Him. He turned his attention to the woman and assured her, "Your faith has saved you. Go in peace."

What the Pharisees deemed an offensive act of emotion, Jesus made into something beautiful and priceless. He replaced her sadness and turmoil with peace.

Jesus longs for your presence no matter what your condition. If you are angry, depressed, hurting, or [you fill in the blank], only He has the ability to release you from your painful distress and replace it with peace. I guarantee He will make ugly emotions into beautiful outpourings of your heart. The more you go to Him, the more you will realize how welcome you are and how unfathomable His love is for you.

A FAITH THAT BREATHES

. . .runs to Jesus for healing. We know we've sinned. Others may know we've sinned. Jesus always knows when we sin, even when we try to shove it aside. But He won't shame us for it. He wants to take it and give us something beautiful

in return. In His presence we experience His unchanging love. We might experience conviction followed by a time of reshaping. He is our Lord and Savior who is eternally perfect. We have every reason to fully trust Him and His promises.

. . .finds unexplainable peace. The situations we encounter that stir up ugly emotions may not change, but we can possess a peace that surpasses human understanding. There's a peace in the core of our being because we have trusted God to be our warrior, provider, and deliverer.

If you know the song, sing with me as we wash His feet with our tears:

> *Draw me close to You. Never let me go.*
> *I lay it all down again to hear You say*
> *that I'm Your friend. . . .*
> *You're all I want. You're all I've ever*
> *needed. You're all I want. Help me*
> *know You are near.*

CHRISTINE GLASS (GLASSBYRD)

When Life Feels Rough— "Hang On"

My husband and I recorded a song titled "Hang On." It's our message to people who are hurting and suffering. They may barely be able to hold on to their idea of God and who He is—and what He means to them.

We're just asking people to hold on. You'll come out of it. With people who love you by your side, you'll be able to make it.

Sometimes we have to stop looking at all the negative stuff in our lives and just make an effort to get outside of ourselves. We get to a point where we have to stop complaining and just do something to solve our problems.

I've had to get up, get outside, and take those very steps. In fact, one time I took a trip to a retreat center called St. Mary's. (It used to be a convent.) I was the only person in the entire place for one night. I needed to be alone and quiet. The next morning, I went for a walk, and everywhere I looked—the sky, the ground, the trees—I sensed the presence of God. He was right there with me. It was truly a new day. I could finally see through all the confusion and emotions inside.

> *Are you having an especially rough time right now? Hang on. . .*
> *Hang on all you children of time*
> *Tired souls, rest your weak and weary mind*
> *There is laughter in the morning*
> *There will be sunlight on your face*
> *So hang on, darkness fades in the light of grace*

There is peace like a river
There is joy like a fountain
There is love like an ocean
Flowing from the hands of God.

the root of bitterness

See to it that no one misses the grace of God

and that no bitter root grows up to

cause trouble and defile many.

—HEBREWS 12:15

Tanya's childhood was marred by abuse. Parents who abused alcohol—and her. Belt buckles. Dark closets. Nightmares and family secrets. Her teenage years brought more of the same, yet no one knew. She had expensive clothes and her own car. Her family was respected in the community—both of her parents were professionals. They had money and prestige. Everyone thought they were a model family.

Her college years were different. Tanya selected a school several states away from home. She felt as if she had finally escaped. No one sent her care packages or cute cards that said, "We miss you." But that was okay. She didn't really want to hear from anyone back home. She stayed on campus on the weekends and spent winter and spring breaks at the homes of her college roommates. She tried to imagine what it would be like to have a loving family to go home to.

One day, while she was studying in the library,

Tanya met a guy named Jeff. Within hours, the two were planning their first date. Two weeks later, they considered themselves a couple. Throughout the next semester, everything Tanya had ever known in her life had changed dramatically. Suddenly, someone loved her, believed in her, and actually treated her like a princess.

Jeff knew God and genuinely talked to Him on a regular basis. He prayed to God about Tanya, and soon she had a desire to know the Lord, too.

Jeff and Tanya began attending a fellowship together and became a part of a cell group. Tanya had never known such love or heard such words of encouragement and hope. The Word of God was beautiful. She especially liked Psalms. Yet building trust and nurturing relationships was difficult for her. She still harbored resentment and hatred for her past—and the pain her family had caused.

Then, one night in cell group, it happened.

She wanted to receive Jesus. She wanted God to be her Father. She realized that Jesus had died for her. Tanya knew she wanted everything her cell group family had talked about: eternal life, forgiveness, love.

If the purpose of her past was to bring her to this moment in time, Tanya felt it was worth what she had gone through. So she prayed and wept tears of repentance. Jesus was now real to her. She felt the love of the Father pouring down on her. Tanya's cell group wrapped their arms of love around her and praised God for the miracle in her life.

Fast-forward five years: Jeff and Tanya are happily

married, and she has grown in God's knowledge and grace. However, even though she and Jeff have a supportive fellowship family, Tanya's relationship with her parents is completely broken. In fact, she does her best not to think about her past.

In the months that followed, Jeff and Tanya became avid hikers. During one of their treks on property Jeff had inherited, they discovered a piece of paradise in the woods—and even began making plans to build a log cabin at the location.

The view was spectacular! Sunsets blazed magenta and scarlet. Deer fed in the valley below. The blue, misty mountains of West Virginia rolled across the horizon.

Over the next few months, Jeff and Tanya drew sketches and discussed how they could build the cabin by themselves. Then the two hiked to the site, hammered wooden stakes into the ground, and attached string to form the layout of the cabin. They planned to have an expansive front porch that faced the overlook of the Blue Mountains.

Anxious to get started, Jeff and Tanya broke ground, slinging shovels full of dirt into a wheelbarrow. Suddenly, they encountered a problem. Jeff hit something solid with his shovel. It just wouldn't budge.

In the exact place the foundation footers were to be dug, a root of massive proportions was discovered beneath the surface. Swinging the mattock as hard as he could and striking the root with all his might, Jeff couldn't even chip it. The thing seemed to be petrified.

As Tanya watched her husband battle the root, a

wave of emotion overtook her. She sat on the ground and continued to watch.

Jeff attacked the root from every angle—then discovered that the main root had a network of smaller roots that were intertwined and gnarled together underground. This is what made the ground rock solid.

Frustrated, Tanya got up and walked away. She simply couldn't give up their plans to build the cabin on this spot with the perfect view. Hiking to rock cliffs high above the valley, she lifted her hands to God and began to pray.

Quietly, God spoke to her: "The root is deep and it has become hard like stone. Even though it is deep and seems impossible to remove, it isn't. You can't remove it alone, but I will remove it for you if you will allow Me to."

It was a moment Tanya would never forget. She felt the awe of God speaking intimately to her. And she knew that her Father wasn't talking about the root Jeff was trying to remove. She knew He was telling her about the petrified root in her heart. She had tried to keep the hate and lack of forgiveness hidden below the surface. Now she wanted it out of her life.

Right there on that ridge, the love of God began to melt her—and tears began to fall. She bowed her head and continued to pray: "I can't deal with this any longer, Lord. Remove this lifelong root of pain and bitterness. Take it away from me and in its place give me love and forgiveness. Heal me from my past. Let me love the family who hurt me. Allow them to see Your love living in me and save them in Jesus' name."

Suddenly, a tremendous weight was lifted from her. God had filled her heart with forgiveness.

• • •

The Lord worked deep in Tanya's heart that day. And by the love and grace of a mighty God, she is being healed and made whole. Today, both roots have been removed. The cabin is complete and sits in the perfect place with the spectacular views. And after years of silence, Tanya and her family are talking. In fact, her parents even visited Jeff and her.

As Tanya and her family sat on her big front porch—the one that overlooks the blue, misty mountains—she was amazed.

The view seems so much better, she told herself.

"Get rid of all bitterness, rage and anger, brawling and slander, along with every form of malice. Be kind and compassionate to one another, forgiving each other, just as in Christ God forgave you" (Ephesians 4:31–32).

A FAITH THAT BREATHES

. . .understands that God wants to work out forgiveness in our hearts. In fact, Christ forgives as we forgive others. Take a good hard look at Matthew 6:14–15. Our Savior's words in these verses are tough—and may even make your knees weak. He tells us that our Father will not forgive our sins if we don't forgive

those who sin against us. *Yikes!* Search your heart: Is there any darkness or resentment that you'll be held accountable for? And as you search your heart, keep this in mind: God's nature *is* forgiveness. (Check out Exodus 34:6–7.) As sinners, we are all "foreigners" and "children of wrath." Yet, according to Ephesians 2, the Lord forgave our rebellion against Him. And Romans 5:8 says that even while we were still rejecting God, Jesus died for us. Get this: Christ looked down at those who nailed Him to the cross and cried out, " 'Father, forgive them, for they do not know what they are doing' " (Luke 23:34).

. . .*knows how to handle anger and bitterness.* In Ephesians 4:26–27, Paul writes, " 'In your anger do not sin': Do not let the sun go down while you are still angry, and do not give the devil a foothold." This passage makes it clear that anger and bitterness aren't usually the problem. It's what these emotions can *lead* to if we don't head them off with God's help. Unsure about what to do? Try this:

- Shift your focus away from the emotion and concentrate on dealing with the situation as Jesus would. Pray. Ask God for help in those volatile moments.

- Strive to settle whatever has made you angry. When you sit and stew about a situation, the whole thing can grow bigger than it has to be. The wise thing to do if you're angry is to deal with it—quickly.

KATHY TROCCOLI
Surviving Life's Valleys

Losing my mother to cancer was one of the hardest things I've had to endure. My mom was an important part of my life. She was really like the woman of my heart. If I didn't have Jesus in my life, I never would have made it through her death.

It happened in October 1992, but it feels like yesterday.

I remember standing outside the operating room of a New York hospital and getting the first dose of bad news.

"We can't save her," a surgeon explained. He gripped my hands and looked me in the eyes. "The cancer has spread through your mom's body. It's a matter of days or months, but she will die."

Fifty million emotions ran through my body at that moment. I was torn. I headed down the hall to a tiny chapel, shut the door, and got on my knees. I knelt silently for a while, feeling as if I was on top of a big mountain. I'd peer over the side and think, *I just can't go on anymore.*

And I remember telling myself, "Kathy, don't do this faith thing anymore, because all you've seen is pain." I mean, when I was a teenager, I experienced the death of my dad—and now my mom! I couldn't believe a loving God would allow this.

I stayed on my knees for what felt like an eternity, struggling with a tug-of-war of emotions. Then Jesus spoke to my spirit as clearly as I'm communicating right now. He said, "Kathy, am I not still God?"

Here I'd been a Christian for many years, and I had to answer that question. I couldn't get up from my knees until I responded to it. I knew if I answered yes, then I had to believe the things He said about Himself—and the promise He gave me.

I thought, *How can I turn away from God during one of the biggest tragedies of my life?* I knew that shaking my fist at Him would be wrong. So, at that moment, I prayed, "God, show me Your love. Give me the strength to make it through this part of my life."

And He did.

On the last day I spent with my mom, I held her hand for six hours. She whispered to me that she wasn't afraid. My sister and I read Psalm 23 to her: "The Lord is my shepherd. . . . Even though I walk through the valley of the shadow of death, I will fear no evil."

All of a sudden, Mom started reciting the passage by heart. That was amazing because I don't remember her ever memorizing Scripture. Then she took her last breath.

But at that moment—while I was at her side crying because she had left me—I knew Jesus was waiting for her with outstretched hands.

(To read more from Kathy Troccoli about God, suffering, and her journey from despair to hope, pick up her book *Am I Not Still God?* published by W Publishing Group.)

crisis control

> "Be still, and know that I am God;
>
> I will be exalted among the nations,
>
> I will be exalted in the earth."
>
> The LORD Almighty is with us;
>
> the God of Jacob is our fortress.
>
> —PSALM 46:10–11

Crisis: a time of great danger or trouble.

Control: to have the power of ruling, guiding, or managing.

The words *crisis control* always make me (Tiffany) think of a reaction to a really bad situation: leadership in the midst of confusion, direction during a time of chaos, a clear thought when nothing else makes sense. Combining these two words, *crisis* and *control,* leads us to believe that we can survive any situation as long as we have properly prepared ourselves ahead of time. It's a belief that a mixture of education, experimentation, and knowledge of science can help us understand and even avoid such situations. And very often, this is exactly what happens.

Knowledge is powerful. Each generation is living longer and healthier lives than its predecessors. Technology is booming. Computers, cell phones, global positioning satellites, and personal digital assistants are improving so quickly that upgrades are already available before you get home with your new purchase. We are benefiting from our parents' and grandparents' emphasis on science and technology. There is hope and excitement as we ponder what is yet to come.

As scientific advances hurtle us into the future, we become more and more dependent upon the comfort and security they offer. How many of us own a cell phone just in case we have a flat tire on a cold rainy night in the middle of nowhere? Why do we have annual physical checkups? Does your home have an alarm system? Have you ever called 9-1-1 during an emergency? Personally, I have experienced all of the above. I am grateful that these awesome inventions are available. They help countless people every day. But what, exactly, are we relying on?

• • •

Most people can recall exactly where they were when they heard that a plane had crashed into one of the World Trade Center towers. Even though the first crash was newsworthy, the story really caught the nation's attention when the second plane hit. All of a sudden, we were thrown into a crisis. What was going on? What were we supposed to do? Everything seemed to stop as millions watched live coverage of innocent victims fighting for their lives. There was mass confusion as panic set in. Thousands were faced with split-second decisions. *Should I stay where I am or try the fire escape? Should I run for cover here or over there? Should I help someone else—or focus on helping myself?*

Meanwhile, our nation's leaders were faced with defending our country from any further attacks. *Should we ground all flights? What action should we take if a 747 isn't responding properly?*

What's more, cell phones weren't working, other airplanes were unaccounted for, the Pentagon was hit, a plane was down in Pennsylvania, the stock market closed, and rescue workers found themselves defending their own lives.

Fortunately, several things also went right that day. Our leaders remained safe, our government functioned, the military performed effectively, and people throughout the world came to our aid. But the moment of horror left us all more than a little shaken. Our sense of security had taken a blow. And it's amazing how quickly our world had changed.

Suddenly, everyone from news anchors to schoolchildren was offering up prayers for the victims and their families. And for a few days, our president didn't receive criticism for using the word *God*. Churches were full, and ministers worked overtime to respond to those in need. When all else failed—people turned to God. Some came in anger and some in confusion but most out of a cry for help.

It all boils down to an issue of trust. What or whom do you run to when the going gets tough?

As we proudly think of how far we have come in such a short period of time, it's easy to rely too heavily on gadgets and systems. Our trust is often misplaced when we depend more on human knowledge than on our Creator. Yet God is jealous.

He has helped us develop the many comforts of modern life, but He does not want them to become a substitute for our trust in Him. What will it take to get our attention? God longs for us to come to Him every day. Don't wait until you are forced out of your comfort zone to lean on God—start building that relationship of trust now.

A FAITH THAT BREATHES

. . . lets go—and lets God! Your heavenly Father wants you to lean on Him daily—during life's storms and when all is "smooth sailing." Commit right now to trust Jesus with your whole heart. Ask Him to help you keep your life grounded in Him, not in man-made security systems.

. . . is being willing to leave your comfort zone. Our comfort zone is the invisible, safe circle we put around ourselves so we don't have to be bothered by anything or anyone. It's a selfish, protective cocoon that keeps us from being all God wants us to be. Besides, clinging to a safe, comfortable life can end up killing the soul.

JILL PHILLIPS
Life after the Wrecking Ball

I recorded a song called "Wrecking Ball," which is about how God uses adversity to build our character, to make us stronger, and to remind us of what we really need.

The Bible tells us that this is all part of the process of finding our identity in Christ and growing in maturity as believers. The second verse of "Wrecking Ball" tells about the Israelites wandering for years in the desert. This Bible story reminds me that God's way of getting me from point A to point B is often very different from what I would expect. Yet He is in control, and His ways can be trusted.

All of my striving and planning and best intentions are never enough to make things unfold the way I want them to happen. We must trust God with the outcome and let Him be in control.

Sometimes we have to let go and trust Him when life isn't easy. And it's during life's hard moments when we discover what we truly believe. Part of knowing Jesus as Savior is recognizing that we need to be saved and turning to Him rather than running away in fear.

a healing touch

How beautiful on the mountains are the feet

of those who bring good news, who proclaim peace,

who bring good tidings, who proclaim salvation,

who say to Zion, "Your God reigns!"

—ISAIAH 52:7

Broken. Lonely. Desperate. The outcast has spent his life on the fringes and his days lived in the shadows. But news travels quickly throughout Galilee—even these forgotten back roads.

The man knows he doesn't have a minute to waste. This is his only hope. He must reach the center of town. Not making it there means destruction. The eternal end to an already pitiful life.

The man covers his hideous physique in a smelly wrap and steps out of a dark alley. Suddenly, he hears a scream. He peeks out from beneath his hood as a woman grabs her child and races to the other side of the street.

"Don't come around here!" yells a person on his right.

"Stay away!" screams another. "You know you're *not* welcome!"

"Get away from us, you unclean man—you *leper.*"

Everywhere he goes, the man faces rejection. But that doesn't stop him. He ignores the painful words and continues to hobble along the hot, dusty road—eventually reaching a crowd at the end of the way.

Standing among the people is the only man who won't reject him—a man who has the power to make him well.

Right there, in the middle of the crowd, is history's most amazing man. A Nazarene. A carpenter. God in the flesh.

Right there—speaking to the broken, the lonely, the desperate—is a man named Jesus.

And when he reaches Jesus, the leper falls on his knees and begs, "If You are willing, You can make me clean."

A most incredible thing happens.

Filled with compassion, Jesus reaches out His hand and touches the man. "I am willing," Jesus says. "Be clean!" And immediately the leprosy leaves the man, and he is cured. (See Mark 1:40–45.)

• • •

"I am willing— be clean!"

These are some of the greatest words spoken in the Bible. Through the Savior's healing touch, sins are forgiven and lives are restored. Through Jesus, people can have peace with their past and peace as they move into their future.

Think about it. How many sections in the hospital would be closed, how many counselors' offices would sit empty, how many bars would go belly up, and how many pharmaceutical companies would go bankrupt if every person would find Christ's healing touch?

Healing. Forgiveness. Peace. Eternity. Our Lord extends His hand and says, "I am willing."

- " 'For God so loved the world that he gave his one and only Son, that whoever believes in him shall not perish but have eternal life' " (John 3:16).

- "If we confess our sins, he is faithful and just and will forgive us our sins and purify us from all unrighteousness" (1 John 1:9).

- "For he himself is our peace, who has made the two one and has destroyed the barrier, the dividing wall of hostility, by abolishing in his flesh the law with its commandments and regulations. His purpose was to create in himself one new man out of the two, thus making peace, and in this one body to reconcile both of them to God through the cross, by which he put to death their hostility" (Ephesians 2:14–16).

A FAITH THAT BREATHES

. . .is cleansed of sins daily. Confession is the key to winning the tug-of-war with sin. It's the answer to making things right again and preventing your old nature from ruining your new life in Christ. You don't have to live with

a huge load of guilt and shame in your life. Tell Jesus all about your sins, tell Him you're sorry, and He'll forgive you.

. . .has found true peace in Christ. It's what everyone needs and longs for deep within their souls. It's why the gospel message of forgiveness of sins is called the gospel of peace. God wants everyone to know His love. He wants to set humanity free and give us eternal peace.

NATALIE WILSON

He Gives "Healing Rest"

I've recorded a song called "Healing Rest." It's drawn from Matthew 9:20–22, the account of Jesus healing a woman who has suffered for years with bleeding:

"Just then a woman who had been subject to bleeding for twelve years came up behind him and touched the edge of his cloak. She said to herself, 'If I only touch his cloak, I will be healed.' Jesus turned and saw her. 'Take heart, daughter,' he said, 'your faith has healed you.' And the woman was healed from that moment."

A mere touch of the Physician's cloak, and the woman was healed. Amazing! And a modern-day analogy would be our becoming healed and whole from whatever issues torment us. I suffered from depression in the last few years, which is a real disease. I'm thrilled to say, God has delivered me!

But during my bouts with depression, I'd sometimes lie awake at night and just cry. I couldn't even find the words to put into prayer. Yet the Lord didn't need words.

He knew what was in my heart as well as all that I was going through. And from my "liquid prayers," He healed me. Through it all I learned that, even when we are at our most tormented state of loss and confusion, He'll meet us where we are and give us a peace that surpasses all understanding.

Because of all that I've been through, I believe the Lord is leading me to help motivate, enlighten, and empower people through my music and ministry. I want those I meet to see that with the Lord they really can achieve their dreams and goals. His healing touch can transform a life.

spiritual break-throughs

> In this you greatly rejoice, though now for a little while
> you may have had to suffer grief in all kinds of trials.
> These have come so that your faith—of greater worth than
> gold, which perishes even though refined by fire—
> may be proved genuine and may result in praise,
> glory and honor when Jesus Christ is revealed.
>
> —1 PETER 1:6–7

Has there ever been a time in your life when you've doubted your Christian walk? Maybe you've wondered if God is truly hearing the prayers you've been praying for weeks, months—maybe even years.

You may even feel trapped in a dungeon and are desperately chipping away at the cold walls—praying that the next strike will bring daylight. You want nothing more than to break through to the other side.

I (Johanna) had a season in my journey when my faith shifted from the nebulous to rock solid.

I had just graduated from college with a B.A. in elementary education. I had been accepted for a position as a teacher in a Christian school on Grand Cayman

Island. I thought living in a highly rated vacation spot would be an incredible experience. *Carpe diem!*

There were several things that needed to happen in order for me to move down there. The two biggest factors were (1) money for a plane ticket for a preliminary visit, and (2) the funds to move everything down there, rent an apartment, and buy a car.

I was sure that if I worked through the entire summer, I could make it.

June flew by, and I couldn't find a job for the summer. I was signed up with five temp agencies, yet not one of them could find me a summer position—each reporting that it was an unusual summer for jobs. Finally, by early July, I had to do what I feared most: turn down the teaching position.

The door was now officially closed. But where would I get a job as a teacher?

College friends in Colorado were persuading me to find teaching positions there—especially so we could all enjoy the mountains together. So I began to send résumés to school districts in the Denver and Colorado Springs areas. After interviewing with four schools, I accepted a position in Colorado Springs. And one Tuesday in mid-August, I packed all my things into our family van and headed to the Rockies.

Teacher orientation and meetings were beginning that Thursday, and the first day of school was ten days away. In the meantime, I was living out of a suitcase in my principal's basement, with all my other things in storage.

Six days before the first day of school, the one possibility of a roommate fell through, and I suddenly felt very alone in a brand-new city, desperately needing a place to live. I decided to drive. I ended up in a Kmart parking lot and just sat there talking to God: "Okay, Lord. You allowed me to come here. It appeared to me that this door was opened. I have to trust in You to provide me a place to live before Monday when kids come to school."

The Lord reminded me that He did pave the way for me to come to Colorado and He would not let me down. The following day, I received an e-mail from a college friend describing his time in Hawaii. In the list of e-mail addresses was one for a girl that I knew was living in Colorado Springs but whom I'd had no way of getting in touch with—until now.

I immediately e-mailed her a brief message, explaining my situation and providing the phone number of where I was staying. I started looking up apartment finder agencies in the phone book. I was literally picking up the phone to start dialing a number when it rang. It was my friend, telling me that she was living in a house with two other girls—and they were currently looking for a fourth roommate. I met the other girls that week, moved in on Saturday, and was ready for the first day of school on Monday.

It took a stressful situation, but after walking through that time, it has since been much easier to trust in the Lord to provide for me in these ways. I find that I no longer worry (as much) about things that I need in order to live. My God will always supply my needs.

• • •

How is your walk with Christ? Are you going through a stressful situation? Have you been laid off from work? Are you looking for something more in life? Does the Lord seem distant to you?

Each of these circumstances is hard, but know this: You are not alone. More important, God really is right there beside you.

Decide now to have victory on the other side as you lean into Christ to help you through. Learn to trust in Him at His word. He will uphold you.

Even when you doubt, He is still there. It is during times of questioning that I feel as if I'm walking through life in a cloudy mist. Yet it is also during these times that God shows me how to trust Him with every area of my life.

Suddenly, spiritual breakthroughs come. Some are small; others are monumental. But each of them is a way in which the Lord reveals Himself. He is more real than any of my words can describe. More real than this book you are holding.

Your circumstances probably aren't easy. Yet the spiritual breakthroughs that come are not a matter of us breaking through to God but rather God breaking through to us.

He is our strong warrior, our pursuer, and the lover of our souls.

...*trusts in the Lord to reveal Himself.* Be patient. God makes Himself known in real ways to our ever-questioning minds. Trust in the promises found in His Word.

...*strives to see with an eternal perspective.* The next time you're filled with doubt, ask yourself this question: Am I willing to throw away what's right and settle for stuff that's wrong (just because I can't feel God in my life right now)? "Do your best to present yourself to God as one approved, a workman who does not need to be ashamed and who correctly handles the word of truth" (2 Timothy 2:15).

"I love you." "I'm proud of you." "I trust you." "I'm there for you." These are powerful words that we desperately need to hear—especially from our families.

I don't know about you, but I need the assurance that my parents are proud of me and happy with my accomplishments. I need to know that they love me in spite of the dumb stuff I may do. Family is important to me.

So, as you can imagine, it was devastating for me when mine broke apart.

When my parents divorced several years ago, it came as a shock to me. I had to constantly tell myself, "Okay, this is the real world we live in, and we need the help and love of Jesus Christ to be able to get through each day."

And even though I knew better, I couldn't help feeling that their breakup was somehow my fault. During tough times like this, our minds begin to play games with us: *If you just would have done "this," maybe your parents would be together and would be happy and everything would be okay.*

I knew in my heart that I wasn't to blame. And as hard as it is to accept, I know for a fact that things happen in life for a reason. I know that my parents still love me and my brothers and sisters. But the pain was real. I simply had to give it all to God and trust Him, step by step.

Through the years, here's what I've learned: Bad things happen in life. But God is still God. He still loves us and will see us through. I can't emphasize it enough: We have to let go and trust Him.

Above all, be real with your family—as well as with others. Don't keep your emotions bottled up inside. Let it out and communicate. Find somebody to lean on. And know this: Tomorrow will be better.

a woman
of purpose

focus your vision

Now listen, you who say, "Today or tomorrow we will
go to this or that city, spend a year there, carry on
business an make money." Why, you do not even know
what will happen tomorrow. What is your life?
You are a mist that appears for a little while and
then vanishes. Instead, you ought to say,
"If it is the Lord's will, we will live and do this
or that." As it is, you boast and brag. All such
boasting is evil. Anyone, then, who knows
the good he ought to do and doesn't do it, sins.

—JAMES 4:13–17

I (Tiffany) was determined to do it. So I swallowed my
pride, mustered up the nerve, and went for it. You see,
I'd always wanted to play chess but had no idea where to
begin—or how to get over the intimidation of learning
this game from someone. To me, chess players always
seemed like cold, intellectual types—deep-thinking, Star-
bucks-sipping, IQ-boasting snobs. I thought this until I
met a couple of chess enthusiasts at work.

Getting the knack of the game was tough at first.

I mean, there was just so much to learn and to memorize before I could even begin my first match. Yet I was determined to discover why so many people dedicate so much of their time to perfecting this game.

For weeks, I watched my coworkers stare silently at the chessboard during their lunchtime matches. (By the way, these guys aren't IQ-boasting snobs; yet they are ruthless competitors who take chess very seriously.)

My friends would spend several minutes of intense thought before they'd move one little piece a mere space or two. Sometimes, in mid-game, one of the players would lean back and disappointedly say, "Ah, you got me. Same time tomorrow?"

Just like that, the game would be over. They were obviously able to look ahead and see how the game would play out. I, on the other hand, was completely lost. Still, I had agreed to stick with my commitment to be a "chess-enthusiast-in-training" for at least two months. Everywhere I went, I carried around my beginner's chessboard and pieces, which conveniently rolled up into one piece. I spent every break, lunch, or downtime familiarizing myself with the various pieces and all of their attributes.

A pawn can do this, a rook can do that; the queen is the most flexible, and the king is to be guarded at all cost. As I met with my chess teacher once a week, he was impressed with my progress and enthusiasm. He convinced me to participate in a chess tournament—as a novice, of course. My first match came and went. So did my second, third, fourth, and so on. At the end of the tourney, I was the only participant who had not won a single game. I was so frustrated. Sheer luck should have let me win at least one match. As my excitement for the game began to wane, I was surprised by the encouragement I received from the other chess players. They all had their own stories of the countless matches they lost before they began to win. They explained that I had to go through this phase in order to become truly familiar with the game.

At the end of my two months of lessons, my instructor reminded me that chess is a game of strategy. "It's easy to get hung up on the rules of engagement," he said, "or even a temporary victory, but that's not what it is all about. With time, you'll begin to see the next move, and the one after that, and the one after that. At that point, you'll truly be playing the game of chess."

It wasn't long before I started to understand what he was talking about. The goal and the rules are set. Every move prompts another move. The game is taken seriously because it requires much dedication and practice to pursue a strategy while simultaneously identifying the opposition's method of attack. One simple move early in a match can easily determine the outcome in the end. In other words, I had to learn to play the game while thinking ahead. Once I figured this out, I began to understand why chess players sit and look at the board for so long before making one simple move. They are trying to play out all of the possible moves mentally.

I have seen the benefits of applying a chesslike strategy to my life. There are times when I feel so overwhelmed and intimidated by life that I lose my focus. During those moments, when I'm just trying to survive the day, it's hard to thoroughly think through some of my decisions. I've come to realize that I've spent most of my life learning rules, customs, and expectations. Now is the time to use this information in order to make better decisions that will lead me closer to my goal.

First, I identified my life goal, which is a growing personal relationship with God. As with chess, every decision I make takes me a step closer or farther away from this goal. It is impossible to know where each battle will take me—but I do know the outcome.

As Christians, we have hope in the future—hope that comes not from how well we play the game but from the love and sacrifice of Jesus Christ. We can rely on this truth as we make life's larger decisions, as well as in our everyday choices. It's important to remember what we have learned, assess our current situation, and mentally play out the possible implications of our choices. This approach brings our daily lives into focus. Our goal is not just something we attain at the end of life; it is a strategy to be played out every day.

A FAITH THAT BREATHES

. . .is focused on something far more important than our plans, goals, and wants. A faith that

breathes has an eternal vision. A committed follower of Christ yearns for the will of God.

. . .is guided by a clear vision of what God wants us to accomplish in life. Ask yourself two fundamental questions: How do I find my place within the body of Christ? How do I pick a profession that is in tune with God's will?

. . .prays with an attitude that seeks the Lord's will. We must place our will into God's plan rather than attempt to force His will into our plans. Spend time in serious reflection and prayer. Ask God for an eternal vision. Ask Him to lead you into His plans for your life.

CHRISSY CONWAY
(ZOEgirl)

A Vision for His "Beautiful Name"

Growing up, I was always looking for somewhere to fit in. I longed for acceptance and a place to belong. However, it always seemed as if the harder I tried, the more I was let down. After I became a Christian, my focus changed drastically. I discovered a whole other side of life through Jesus. It was then that I began to realize how temporary this world is and how permanent eternity is. I found myself less concerned with fitting in with the world and more concerned with belonging to God.

Christ is truly the only One who knows my thoughts before I think them. He's the only One who knew every day of my life before I even took my first breath. No one else but God could ever love me and accept me for who I am the way that He can. He's the only One who truly gets me—the only One whom I want to serve and follow with every breath I have.

We recorded a song titled "Beautiful Name" that states every person's mission as a Christian and is meant to challenge and encourage us in our walk. Matthew 28:19–20 sums up this mission: " 'Therefore go and make disciples of all nations, baptizing them in the name of the Father and of the Son and of the Holy Spirit, and teaching them to obey everything I have commanded you. And surely I am with you always, to the very end of the age.' "

We have a calling on this earth. And for the sake of the name of Jesus, we will stop at nothing until it is fulfilled.

discover your genius

"The fear of the LORD is the beginning of wisdom,
and knowledge of the Holy One is understanding.
For through me your days will be many,
and years will be added to your life.
If you are wise, your wisdom will reward you;
if you are a mocker, you alone will suffer."

—PROVERBS 9:10—12

Humankind has always had an insatiable desire to probe the unexplored and find the undiscovered. History abounds with examples:

- Archimedes discovering his principle concerning mass and weight
- Amelia Earhart exploring the realms of aviation
- Columbus discovering America
- Sigmund Freud exploring the human mind
- Alexander Fleming discovering penicillin
- Neil Armstrong exploring the moon

The excitement of discovery can eclipse all other events in a person's life. Think of the explorers crying out "Land ho!" as they sighted the New World. Think of prospectors uncovering gold in the streams of California during the gold rush days.[21]

Christians can also experience the thrill of discovery. They have within their grasp a key that can unlock unimaginable spiritual awakening. By reading and studying the Scriptures, the eternal and abiding Word of God, believers can explore absolute truth. And in the process, they can discover abundant life, true fulfillment, real genius.

In the sixty-six books of the Bible, God has enclosed exciting insights, nuggets of gold waiting to be uncovered, precious gems that will never perish. Take the Bible in your hand. Open it. Read it. Study it. Explore it. Discover it. Do it daily.

• • •

If you're like most busy women, you've probably noticed that your times with the Lord too often become rushed. You fly through a few verses, then whisper a quick prayer before heading out the door. But stop and consider this: The core things in life—especially your relationship with God—simply cannot be rushed. The Lord wants you to slow down, disconnect from the world, and immerse yourself in truth. He wants you to savor His Word daily.

So why is reading and studying the Bible so important? Because Scripture strengthens your Christian mind. The New Testament instructs us to be transformed by the renewing of our minds (see Romans 12:2).

If you don't know what your faith is built on, how can you defend your faith when students and teachers or people in the workplace don't take it seriously? Get excited about saturating your mind with the wisdom of God and standing for truth in a world that denies it.

Keep the name of Jesus on your lips and His Word in your heart, and you won't go wrong. Commit yourself to Him and your genius will blossom. But if you settle for man-made genius—the knowledge and truth of the world—you'll be eternally disappointed.

In the words of author Max Lucado, "One source of man's weariness is the pursuit of things that can never satisfy; but which one of us has not been caught up in that pursuit at some time in our life? Our passions, possessions, and pride—these are all *dead* things. When we try to get life out of dead things, the result is only weariness and dissatisfaction."[22]

The choice is yours. Love God with all your heart, mind, and soul. Keep Jesus as your No. 1 passion and priority in life. Delight in the Lord. Do these things, and He will give you the desires of your heart. You will discover your genius.

A FAITH THAT BREATHES

. . .is careful to not grow numb and mindless.

Ultimately, any true pursuit of God will lead us to God because there's only one truth. But as the Bible warns, "See to it that no one takes you captive through hollow and deceptive philosophy, which depends on human tradition and the basic principles of this world rather than on Christ" (Colossians 2:8).

. . . *steers clear of "cultural Christianity."* Stay grounded in God and "check your pulse" from time to time. Don't be afraid to ask yourself some hard questions: *Is my faith getting too comfortable? Is it becoming watered down? Am I compromising? Am I pursuing religion or relationship? Is my faith in Jesus Christ based on the absolute truth of the Bible or on traditions invented by well-meaning believers? Why do I believe what I claim to believe? Does my talk match my walk?*

. . . *knows that prayer, along with Bible reading, will unlock a believer's genius.* Take an afternoon, a weekend, or an hour a day for a month—whatever you need—and pray about your gifts and talents. Pray about God's will for your life. Then listen to His answers. Focus on His voice and direction.

SARA SADLER

What I Was Born to Do

I'm a third-generation musician, so you could say that music is in my blood. My vocal gifts came naturally by way of my grandmother, who was an accomplished musician. My lyrical abilities and love of words came from my father (and songwriting partner), Gary Sadler. He is a recognized worship leader and the writer of the songs "Ancient of Days" and "Lord Over All."

At age nine, I wrote my first song, "I Will Pray," which landed on a children's album that was recorded by Integrity Music. More than a decade later, I'm still writing songs and singing, which I'm convinced is what I was born to do. So, what's my message? Simply this: God loves us.

So many people today are consumed in the wrongs of the world. They feel victimized and cheated. Living a ho-hum life, being the victim of circumstances—that's not for me. I know that I can take what's on my plate and make it as good as it can be.

In our society, there is this "you-owe-me-something" mentality, and I don't agree with that. Nobody owes us anything. There are a lot of takers and not a lot of givers. I want to give more than I take. After all, consider what Christ gave to us: His life.

I love life. And life is about people and relationships. I think that many of my songs reflect the relationships I have and how I view them. I've had a lot of great Christian influences growing up, mainly thanks to my parents for raising me in a Christian home. When you have someone in your life who walks with Christ, His beauty shines through them and it compels you to want to be that way, too.

A song I recorded, "Running into You," comes to mind. I listen to it over and over. It makes me feel good, and I think the verses paint a picture we've all seen:

"There are days and there are nights when I just
want to run from the heartache
From the mistakes, far from everyone
If I'm falling or if I'm flying I keep seeing You."

To me, that is raw emotion everyone can relate to. It says, "No matter how much I don't think I need You, Lord, I know inside that I do. Every corner I turn, You are there. It's love, regardless."

As Christians, we are called to love each other and to speak into people's lives. I think it's important to be artistic but in a way that somebody can understand. If a song is not speaking into people's lives, you've almost failed as a songwriter. I want to reach people with my music.

unlock a dream

To man belong the plans of the heart, but from the LORD comes the reply of the tongue. All a man's ways seem innocent to him, but motives are weighed by the LORD. Commit to the LORD whatever you do, and your plans will succeed. The LORD works out everything for his own ends— even the wicked for a day of disaster. The LORD detests all the proud of heart. Be sure of this: They will not go unpunished. Through love and faithfulness sin is atoned for; through the fear of the LORD a man avoids evil. When a man's ways are pleasing to the LORD, he makes even his enemies live at peace with him. Better a little with righteousness than much gain with injustice. In his heart a man plans his course, but the LORD determines his steps.

—PROVERBS 16:1–9

What is a dream? Is it some bizarre fantasy we have as we sleep that makes no sense when we wake in the morning? Or is it a vision of something greater pursued by great leaders such as Martin Luther King, Jr., George Washington, or Mother Teresa?

These are usually the two extremes that jump into our minds when we think of dreams. What if dreams were something far more personal? What if they were the true desires of our heart? In the words of author John Eldredge (in his book, *Dare to Desire*), "What if those deep desires in our hearts are telling us the truth, revealing to us the life we were meant to live?"[23]

Dreams are sometimes associated with the bizarre or the lofty. But we all have them. We call them goals, aspirations, or life plans. But these are the dreams that come from within. They are at the core of our being. We dream as differently as we are created. Even as we are influenced by our families, childhood, education, media, and relationships, we tend to return to our childhood dreams. Our desires resurface time and time again.

For me (Tiffany), my earliest aspiration was to be a firefighter. I proudly announced this decision at the age of six after looking at a cool red fire truck for sale on the back of a cereal box.

Our house was also down the road from a fire-fighting training facility. As these brave men performed their drills, the fire engines would scream past our house with their lights ablaze and sirens howling. All of the children would get excited and race to their front yards to wave and cheer them on. This childhood ritual may seem a little silly now, but it helped to form an image of a hero in my mind. But when I said, "I'm going to be a firefighter," my friend quickly spoke up and informed me that only boys became firefighters. Even though I was a little embarrassed, I responded by saying, "So, I'll be one anyway."

Needless to say, I never became a firefighter—but I have always traveled an unusual path. I believe my early proclamation was more of an insight to the type of goals I would pursue in life rather than an actual career choice.

As a woman, I have worked in radio, served in the armed forces, and worked in film and video production. My hobbies include hiking, camping, photography, and international travel. I have driven across country alone several times. I just seem to be drawn to the more physical and sometimes edgy pursuits. But that is the woman who God created me to be. I'm also happily married and a full-time mom. Motherhood alone has proven to be the most demanding and rewarding challenge of my life.

These aren't contradictory dreams; they are just unique to me.

One of my closest friends in the world leads a completely different life. She isn't into electronics, has no interest in the military, and prefers to travel in luxury. Now in her mid-thirties, she has decided to pursue her dream of becoming a nurse. She is back in school and loving every minute of it. We appear to be complete opposites. I believe the key to our lifelong friendship is the support we have always shown each other when it comes to our dreams. We just seem to have the same basic outlook on life: We are uniquely created by God and should therefore live that way. Own it. Pursue it. Love it.

• • •

" 'I have come that they may have life, and that they may have it more abundantly' " (John 10:10 NKJV).

Are you living the life that God has chosen for you? In the midst of responsibility and duty, we often suppress the desires of our heart. We have been created to live, love, and praise our God. Through prayer and honest self-evaluation, the desires of our heart will become clear. The pursuit of these God-given desires will draw us closer to Him and help us to define who and whose we are.

Close your eyes and imagine three desires of your heart. Don't think about it or rationalize your wishes—just dream. Does your life in any way represent those dreams? Are the items on your list consistent? Do you identify a theme among your wishes? How do your dreams compare to those you had as a child? When was the last time you asked God to help you clarify your dreams?

A FAITH THAT BREATHES

. . . *focuses on the gifts and talents that God has given us.* Ask the Lord to reveal what His "good, pleasing and perfect will" for your life looks like (Romans 12:2).

. . . *shares dreams with others.* Talk with any family or friends who might serve as a mentor. Let people know about your dreams and aspirations. Their input will be valuable in finding the life pursuit that will best shape the person inside you.

ALYSSA BARLOW OF BARLOWGIRL

God Took Away a Dream—and Gave Back a Better One

Becoming a superstar is a big deal in our culture right now. Even I had dreams of one day starring on Broadway. (I love dancing and acting.) Yet God said to me, "What would happen if you gave those dreams to Me—and I didn't give them back to you?"

I thought, *Are You joking?* But I just couldn't deny it: In my heart I sensed Him telling me to quit theater.

I went through a hard time of actually being angry with God and thinking He was so mean for wanting to take my desires away from me. Yet the more I resisted Him, the more miserable I began to feel. And during this struggle, I fell down some stairs and was diagnosed with a disease called reflex sympathetic dystrophy (RSD). Doctors told me that I would never walk normally again and that I'd end up in a wheelchair. Everything in a matter of two days was taken away from me—my dreams of dance, of Broadway. So here was this girl who had been a "good little church girl" for most of her life now struggling with her faith and unsure if she wanted to serve God at all.

Then it happened: a miracle. God began to change my heart—and mend my body. I slowly regained full ability to walk. And suddenly my lifelong dream to make it big on Broadway didn't seem so important. I soon began to realize that His call on my life was not to be an actress or to play a role on stage. Instead, God wanted me to be real with Him and with myself. He asked me to trust Him with everything.

Little by little, God began to stir a passion inside of me—a passion for serving Him. I didn't know how my life was going to turn out—whether I was going to be a missionary or an artist. But I knew I had a purpose—His purpose. A short time later, BarlowGirl was born. God gave back to me even better dreams than I ever imagined.

I share this whole experience in a song we recorded called "Surrender." This tune is my life story. It's a cry to God: "I don't know what You have for me." All I heard Him say was, "Surrender. I promise I'll take care of you."

Here's what I want people to know about me: I am a testimony of God asking me to surrender my dreams so He can bless me with something better. I'm so excited about where He has me right now. And I know that this isn't the end. It's actually just the beginning of what He's going to accomplish in my life.

don't waste your talent

There are different kinds of gifts, but the same Spirit.

There are different kinds of service, but the same Lord.

There are different kinds of working,

but the same God works all of them in all men.

—1 CORINTHIANS 12:4–6

Life rocks for world champion climber Tori Allen. This young woman has set her goals high—and isn't about to waste her God-given talent.

Tori's formative years were spent in West Benin, Africa, where her family served as missionaries. Tori's mom taught literacy and business to the local women, while her dad focused on building leadership in their church through Bible studies and discipleship.

During her teen years, Tori's family moved back to the United States. That's when this natural athlete was introduced to rock climbing. She spotted a climbing wall at a sporting goods store and begged her dad to let her try. It was love at first climb!

To date, her natural ability has gained international recognition and set world records. In her own words, Tori shares her story, as well as some thoughts about the gifts and talent God gives us all.

I love climbing because it's fun and I love heights. It's definitely a gift from God. Everybody has gifts and talents and should be using them as best they can. My gift just happens to be scampering up the side of a rock face. I plan to climb as long as it's fun. I'll know when it's time to move on to some other gift God has given me.

Whether an injury or a better opportunity comes, I'll follow God's lead on that. I strive to always take the high road with decisions. In the short run, it might stink for me, but in the long run, it may be better. I've always gone above and beyond in everything. "I can't" isn't in my dictionary. "If" isn't an option, either. It's "when" I'm going to do things. God gives me discernment to make decisions.

I've done my best to never be blinded by the spotlight. I do my best to encourage others. At competitions, I throw a stuffed monkey doll to the crowd after a successful climb, just for fun. In my local community, I volunteer to teach others about the beauty of the climbing world, and I speak out as an advocate for the preservation of outdoor climbing areas. My tithes have gone to friends in Benin to build a better house for them.

My grandma sent boxes to us every month in Africa, and we'd give away the toys that she'd included. When I came back to the States, everybody had everything. I started saving my *kid's meal toys to send to African children. Then I started saving my allowance and baby-sitting money for postage. I thought I'd keep sending these boxes and call them Happy Boxes. Every day you wake up, think about the decisions you'll make to change the world. If you want people to get closer to God, then live like that.*

• • •

As this book went to press, Tori was a full-time high school honors student in Indiana, not to mention a two-sport athlete: a rock climber and a pole-vaulter.

Her top-notch abilities and positive attitude have earned her the respect of pro athletes worldwide, not to mention lots of media attention. To date, she has appeared on the *Morning Show* and the *Today Show*—and has been featured in *Sports Illustrated, ESPN* the magazine, *The New York Times,* and *YM.* Tori has also been named as the youngest of the "Top 25 Athletes under 25" by *Outside Magazine.*

In Tori's words, "Everybody has gifts and talents and should be using them as best they can." How has God gifted you?

Are you serving Him with your abilities? And like Tori, have you erased the words "I can't" from your dictionary? Do you dream dreams, set goals, and declare *"when* I use this talent and fulfill this plan"—instead of saying, *"if* I do this"?

We're all part of the Body of Christ—the Church—that Paul tells us about in 1 Corinthians 12:12–31. And though we are many members of the Body, there is still one Body, one cause—one Creator we serve. Paul explained, "The body is a unit, though it is made up of many parts; and though all its parts are many, they form one body. So it is with Christ. . . . Now you are the body of Christ, and each one of you is a part of it" (1 Corinthians 12:12, 27).

While God bestows an amazing array of gifts upon His creation, He has chosen each member to make a unique contribution to the Body. In other words, the Body needs each member, and each member needs the Body. And each member is called to be loyal to her Head, the Master, to fulfill His purpose for her life, to perform the functions that keep the Body vibrantly alive and in step with the Head, the living Head, our Lord Jesus Christ.

Successful people have found their place within the Body. They don't waste their God-given talent on pursuits that counter God's will. Guided by a clear personal vision of what Christ wants them to accomplish in life, they possess an accurate and precise picture of the work that expresses them best. As a result, these individuals experience profound and lasting benefits: reduced stress, more balance, a more productive career, and a more satisfying life.

Are these your desires as well? Then stop wasting your talent. Tune in to the gifts God has given you, tune in to His will—and get going!

. . .knows the secret to success. You'll find your unique place in this world—and ultimately, true fulfillment—if you fit yourself into what God wants for you rather than trying to fit God into what you want for yourself.

. . .sets goals. A goal is the end toward which you direct your effort. Similar to scoring a goal in sports, you'll strive to attain them and will find joy in achieving them. And as soon as you reach one goal, you can't wait to reach the next one. Don't be afraid to set goals for your life. Remember these three things about a life goal: It's concrete (you can put it into words), it's measurable (you can monitor your progress), and it's attainable (you can reasonably complete it).

NATALIE GRANT

Music Is My Mission

Growing up, I wanted to be a missionary and a nurse. But I can't stand the sight of blood, so I quickly learned that the medical field wasn't for me. I ended up studying elementary education in college. (I wanted to be a first-grade teacher.)

So, how did I go from wanting to be a nurse, then a teacher, to becoming a contemporary Christian music artist? I'm still trying to figure that out!

Actually, I grew up singing in my church. We had an incredible youth program. Then, a musical group named Truth came to my church in Seattle, and I auditioned for them.

Truth—made up of six singers and a full band—has helped start the careers of so many CCM artists: Steve Green, 4 Him, Point of Grace—just to name a few. It was during my time with Truth that God called me to launch out as an artist.

I ended up moving straight from the Truth bus to Nashville. God has given me the gift of music—and I'm determined to serve Him with it.

What's my advice for other up-and-coming artists? Ask yourself why you want to be a musician. Is it for the fame? Do you want to be a pop star—an "American Idol," so to speak? Or is God directing you into this line of work? If you're choosing to do it as a ministry career, know this: It's not a lifestyle of the rich and famous. It's very tough but rewarding work.

I'm a CCM artist because that's who God has called me to be. And when He calls you to something—go for it with all your heart!

career vs. calling

And whatever you do, whether in word or deed,

do it all in the name of the Lord Jesus,

giving thanks to God the Father through him.

—COLOSSIANS 3:17

At 6 A.M., the alarm rings.

Oh how Susan hates to get up and go to work. It's the same thing every day: work, break, work, lunch, work, break, work, and then—ah, finally—time to go home. For her, life begins at 5 P.M. That's when she enjoys a meal with her boyfriend, followed by a movie—or maybe something decent on TV.

She savors these few hours of sanity. But work— "Oh, how it's a purely dreadful pursuit. But I do it for a paycheck. I do it for those few hours of sanity."

In an apartment across the hall lives Susan's neighbor, Elisabeth. Her alarm goes off at 6 A.M., too, and she works at the same place as Susan. But Elisabeth loves what she does. She's convinced that her work is important for the success of the company. She works with enthusiasm and pride, finding personal satisfaction in every detail she completes. Evenings are fun, too, adding variety to her life.

"I have much to be thankful for," Elisabeth says with a smile. "God has blessed me with a great career—an awesome sense of purpose and fulfillment. All that I do, I approach with my whole heart, as if working for the Lord."

• • •

Two women, two jobs—yet two very different perspectives. Which one best describes you? Or to put it another way, which attitude do you demonstrate as you go about your daily tasks?

There's a big difference between working for a paycheck and working with a purpose. While having a positive attitude is an important factor, the key ingredients are (1) discovering your God-given gifts and talents, (2) committing them to the Lord, and (3) using them to their fullest.

God has given each one of us the ability to be remarkable at something. He wants us to find joy and satisfaction in our daily tasks. But for far too many people, "interests" and "work" are two entirely separate subjects. If all you see is the money earned and what little you can do with it, you will feel empty and unfulfilled.

Vow to be different. Examine carefully what you're drawn to in life—the pursuits that fascinate you. Then take the brave steps toward your dreams. And regardless of your job now—or what you end up doing in the future—if you consider work as God's gift to you, your life will become filled with "gladness of heart." Begin your day with this prayer, "God, establish the work of my hands today." (See Psalm 90:17.)[24]

...doesn't just blend in with the masses. When it comes to your career, don't just settle for a paycheck. Instead, stand out in the crowd and pinpoint the kind of job that gives you meaning and purpose. "Use your imagination as you think about employment possibilities," says the manager of human resources at Coca-Cola in Atlanta. "Of course, we hire people who enjoy our products."

...takes Christ into the workplace. In our scenario above, the biggest difference between Susan and Elisabeth does not lie in the working hand but in the attitude of the heart. Susan viewed her job as a necessary evil—a means merely to make money for the nonworking moments of life. Elisabeth, on the other hand, found purpose and meaning within her work. She used her job to serve God and her fellow man.

...knows that laziness can kill meaning, purpose, direction. Avoid it. It can dim the focus in your work and blur the meaning in what God has called you to do. It can drain all the vitality out of your life. Ask God to remind you what a wonderful gift work really is.

. . .maintains a healthy attitude about knowledge, position, and self-image. Okay, let's look into the future a bit. Let's say you've landed a prestigious position and everybody is now looking up at you. Don't let it go to your head. In fact, as your dreams become reality, you'd be wise to keep your feet firmly planted on the ground—and your head out of the clouds.

In his book *The Imitation of Christ*, Thomas à Kempis, author and Augustinian monk, offers some suggestions on how we should live:

> *You may know a lot, yes, but there's also a lot you don't know. "Don't be a wiseacre," wrote Paul to the Romans (11:20). Admit you're not omniscient. And when it comes to standing in line, what about the people ahead of you? Apparently, they know more than you do. Get used to knowing less than God. Get used to the middle of the line. That's where you belong.*
>
> *What's the most profound, and yet the most practical, lesson you can learn? That you look like an ant! What's the deepest wisdom and yet the highest perfection? That you are an ant! Have no illusions about yourself—that's what Paul laid upon the Romans (11:20). Hold high opinions only about others.*[25]

JOY WILLIAMS

How to Be Successful in Life

When I was offered a record deal at fourteen, it virtually dropped in my lap. After praying about it, I didn't feel that it was what God wanted me to do. Turning down that opportunity made me look like a fool. But I said, "I know God has good plans for me. And I trust that they're going to fit the pattern of 1 Corinthians 2:9–10, ' "No eye has seen, no ear has heard, no mind has conceived what God has prepared for those who love him—but God has revealed it to us by his Spirit." ' "

Over the next couple of years, God helped me begin to grow. I'm not just here to sing Christian music. I'm here to talk with people about the amazing way that Christ can transform their lives—and about how He's transformed mine. If people haven't met Christ, I hope they'll see who He is and how badly they need Him in their lives.

In all honesty, I don't view what I do as a career. Yet the word *ministry* doesn't quite fit, either. (It sounds so formal!)

What did Christ do? He went around with His disciples to different towns and told them about who He was. I'm just a disciple praying that God will allow me to help others become disciples. If you want to say my emphasis is on the ministry, I sure hope so. Careers come and go, but eternal fruit will last.

So, what success tip am I learning from God? This: I've always been a people-pleaser, yet the Lord is telling me, "The only person you need to please is Me. If you're walking My way, then that's the way that I will bless."

It's not always the easy path, yet it's the high road. And while it's difficult to travel at times, following God's path leads to true fulfillment.

knowing God's will

"I will give you the treasures of darkness,

riches stored in secret places,

so that you may know that I am the LORD,

the God of Israel, who summons you by name."

—ISAIAH 45:3

The hidden riches of secret places. . .

Does God tell you secrets? Has He ever whispered knowledge into your spiritual ear—a secret that gives you special wisdom about a situation?

Perhaps He has spoken to your heart to help you discern the truth or gain perspective about a relationship. Maybe His prompting has sensitized you to prepare for something that was about to happen, that is, so you wouldn't be caught off guard.

These are only a few of the ways in which God whispers secrets to us.

Has the Spirit ever revealed something funny to you? Often, into those who have "ears" to hear, He speaks a little private humor that only His understanding of a person or situation can bring. At times, He may call to our attention tiny tidbits of truth about ourselves that we keep very private—our silliness, our secret goofs. And with a childlike joy and amusement, He helps us laugh at ourselves in His presence.

Private jokes with God—who would have thought?

So, to what kind of woman does God tell His secrets? To what kind of woman would God choose to reveal the hidden riches of secret places?

To the kind of woman reading this book. To you, actually.

•••

You are God's beloved. You carry the mark of His Son, who has sought you at a great price and placed upon you great value. You are the jewel set in His crown. Your heart and your very life belong to Him. Your surrender to His loving embrace will bring whispers of intimacy and revelation that can only come from His heart—communicated directly to your heart.

What would cause the Creator of the universe to whisper to you His secrets? Often, He will speak to you in response to your love for Him. He desires nothing more than for you to join your heart with His and fall in love. Remember, God is not a man that He should lie. He does not betray us. He has given all He had and all He was so that you could know that He loves you with an intimacy that surpasses all others.

Through Jesus, God has betrothed Himself to you. In Hosea 2:19, He has promised, " 'I will betroth you to me forever; I will betroth you in righteousness and justice, in love and compassion.' "

He does not change like the wind, and He will not

change His mind about loving you and calling you to follow in His footsteps. He has promised never to leave you or forsake you.

The One who loves you speaks wisdom to your spirit and leads you in the way you should go. Regardless of what path your feet may be on, His voice is constantly speaking (whether we listen or not), saying, " 'This is the way; walk in it' " (Isaiah 30:21). The Lord *wants* to tell us His secrets.

So, what can you do to deepen your relationship with Him so you can be in a position to hear Him speak to your heart? There are several steps you can take. . .

A FAITH THAT BREATHES

. . .*sows the Holy Scriptures into your heart to strengthen your ability to discern truth.* Outside of His truth, our hearts fall into darkness and sin, which block His voice. We cannot know the will of God if we do not become intimately acquainted with His Word. Jesus is the Living Word and the Living Truth. To know Jesus is to have a constant stream of truth flowing into your soul. You must know Him and walk with Him and open your spirit to the life-giving food in the Holy Scriptures. Immerse yourself in the Holy Scriptures and ask God to reveal Himself to you through them. Remember, Jesus is the Truth.

. . .spends time adoring Him and allowing Him to love you. Do not say to yourself, "I am ugly and unclean and unlovable and unholy." Instead, say to yourself, "I belong to Jesus and He is mine and I am His." In the Song of Solomon, the woman sings, "I am my beloved's and my beloved is mine." As children, we sang that song and followed it with, "His banner over me is love." Remember God is your covering. Hide yourself in Him. Separate yourself to Him. Belong to Him completely.

. . .allows the Holy One to sing over you, to dance over you, to rejoice over you with love. In Zephaniah, we read about God dancing over us with joy. Learn to bask in His favor and total acceptance and forgiveness. Strive to enjoy His presence!

. . .asks for direction in small things. Then, be obedient—regardless of how uncomfortable it may make you feel at first. If you learn to be obedient in the small things, He will give you greater and greater revelation. Rick Joyner once said, "With the greater anointing comes the greater specificity." As God "anoints" you with the oil of His Spirit, your sweet obedience to Him positions you to receive greater and more specific revelation. As with everything in the kingdom of God,

faithfulness in small things always leads to greater things.

. . .*takes every request to God—both big and small.*
Are you one of those people who asks God for a good parking spot at the mall, then worries that it may have been too trivial of a thing to ask Him? I (Tess) am one of those women. But I feel God told me: "It doesn't anger Me that you ask for such a small thing. After all, if you can't listen well enough to hear small instructions, how can I trust you to hear Me when I need to give you more complicated directions? Start small, and as you learn to hear Me tell you where to park, I'll begin to tell you which direction to take your life." And this is the truth. God takes the trivial things in our lives and makes them into building blocks of relationship and trust, laying the foundation for obedience and revelation in our lives.

PAIGE LEWIS (PAIGE)

God Has an Awesome Plan for YOU!

Through my platform as an artist, here's what I want to tell people: "Look, God has an awesome plan for your life, and it's so much better than you can figure out on your own."

Surrender every dream, every desire—everything to God. He is powerful and incredibly excited about using us in this world to make a difference. But it requires that we give up control in order for Him to reveal His power through us.

I wrote the lyrics to the song "Jonah" during my fifth-period class one day in high school. As I headed down the hallway, one of my friends handed a note to me. It contained a very cool verse from the Book of Jonah: " 'Those who cling to worthless idols forfeit the grace that could be theirs' " (Jonah 2:8).

I went to class and did my best to look as though I was working on my assignment. In truth, I was writing the words to the song. It talks about taking away the things that keep us from God—in order to see Him more clearly.

When it comes to God's will for my life, this is what I'm striving to do. I want to cut through the things of this world and see Him—and hear Him—more clearly. I have found that the only way to truly live for God is to live in God. I find the strength I need to press on when I hide myself in Him.

How? Storing God's Word in my heart is a concept that I've learned about since I was six. But it's not until recently that I have realized just how important it is to know Scripture and make it real in my life. (For more on this topic, read Psalm 119.)

My advice: Don't wait any longer to get real with God.

He is just waiting for us to look to Him so He can use us in amazing ways. It is never too early to get serious about living for God and following Him no matter what people think. "Do not conform any longer to the pattern of this world, but be transformed by the renewing of your mind. Then you will be able to test and approve what God's will is—his good, pleasing and perfect will" (Romans 12:2).

boldly going where God leads

"For I know the plans I have for you," declares the LORD,

"plans to prosper you and not to harm you,

plans to give you hope and a future."

—JEREMIAH 29:11

"To boldly go where no man has gone before."

Sound familiar? If you're into classic TV episodes of *Star Trek,* the corners of your mouth undoubtedly turned up into a knowing grin. The wheels of your imagination began to spin as your mind flashed with images of aliens, newly discovered civilizations, and countless life-and-death situations that were fought and won—all within sixty minutes!

I (Vanessa) have always loved a good story—whether it unfolds on the big screen or in the pages of a book. I especially enjoy the kind in which good triumphs over evil—an adventure in which an ordinary person finds himself in extraordinary circumstances, ultimately becoming the hero who overcomes impossible odds.

With movies and novels, you know how long the

conflict will last, right? All you have to do is glance at your watch or check the number of pages left in the book. But life is not like this.

The real world doesn't always provide you with a last-minute solution, hidden until you have a need for it. Life doesn't always leave you feeling triumphant and fulfilled. Sometimes it does, but often it just doesn't, no matter how hard you work at it.

The truth is, you and I need the Savior. As mere mortals—with no superpowers or futuristic gadgets to protect us—we need the One who is omniscient, larger than life, the ultimate Hero. Yet we are often afraid of stepping out in faith because we have learned not to have faith—in life, in circumstances, or even in ourselves.

But what about our faith in God? How far will our faith really lead us?

• • •

As a Christian—as a committed follower of Jesus—you know that the Lord leads you through some rocky roads. Yet Jesus never took the comfy paths when He was here in the flesh. And He doesn't take them now in the person of the Holy Spirit, your guide. The truth is, if you want to stay in your comfort zone, you can, but you'll lose sight of Him very quickly as He moves on—reaching out to those who need Him.

Instead, He calls us to boldly follow Him everywhere He goes.

You and I have a mission. And if we choose to accept it, we can change lives for eternity. This is actually what we were made for. We will never find fulfillment in life unless we find our mission, our calling, our purpose. It's our job to love God and to serve Him boldly.

Come to think of it, this is what the human heart yearns for. We can see it all around us: TV shows, movies, and books—stories that compel us to step out in faith, to do the impossible, and to strive to become overcomers.

We have a longing to step out into the unknown while still having the assurance that all will work out for the best, just as God guarantees it will. There's a yearning in each of us to follow a powerful, almighty God who is truly good and truly loving—who will provide us with that last-minute way out—every time, even when life closes all the doors.

But many times we hold back because of fear and uncertainty, because we don't want to be left out on the limb if God doesn't come through.

Yet as we go, without hesitation, isn't He there with us—guarding and guiding us? Jesus said, "I will never leave you or forsake you."

The simple, yet profound truth is that if we trust God to be who He claims to be, then we can go and speak and do all He calls us to accomplish. And we can do it boldly, with the assurance that God will make a way for us. He will protect us until the end. He will never leave us. Committed followers of Christ have tested this time and time again and know it to be true. He is faithful.

A FAITH THAT BREATHES

. . . *strives for real adventure.* A life lived in Jesus can never be dull or boring. It is filled with constant adventure. Every day holds new and wonderful promise and surprise. And when all is said and done—when we stand before Him on Judgment Day, we can look forward to seeing Him smile at us and say, "Well done, good and faithful servant."

. . . *isn't a solo servant.* We just can't follow Jesus on our own. We weren't created that way. The Bible says we are a body in Christ. A hand can't separate itself from the body and exist by itself. It needs the rest of the body to survive.

. . . *chooses friends carefully.* Someone once said, "Show me your friends, and I'll show you your future." Good advice. Be careful about the environment you put yourself in—and the people you surround yourself with. We fool ourselves into thinking we can hang out with a certain crowd and not be affected. But scripture is very clear on this matter: "Resist the devil, and he will flee from you" (James 4:7). True Christian friends build each other up. They say, "I think God created a pretty awesome creature when He made you." Bottom line: Develop relationships with people who share your convictions and support each other.

. . . *reflects God's values.* Christ wants us to care for other people just as He cares for all of His creatures. He wants us to be compassionate to hurting people just as Jesus shows us compassion. He wants us to treat others with love just as He loved us by sending His Son to die for us. That's His claim on us: We as human beings are His living story.[26]

ALISON OGREN
(CLEAR)
Why I Do What I Do

To me, being a musician is not just a way to make a living or just something I do to pass the time. I believe that God created me to sing. There's a familiar sense of peace that comes over me when I sing, and I know that I'm right where God wants me to be.

I had been accepted to Belmont University's School of Music in Nashville and Bethel College in Minnesota. I knew that going to college was the most practical thing for me to do, but in my heart, all I wanted was to minister to people through music. I think God made that decision for me when we were offered a record contract with Ardent. I knew right away that God's hand had led me to that place and all I had to do was follow Him.

We've had our struggles as a band, but there is still joy in the pain. We know that God has brought us this far and that He has a purpose for us. My hope is that through my decision to serve God with my voice, other people will be drawn to His presence. I know that as long as I remain faithful in my personal life to what God calls me to do, He will be faithful to fulfill His purpose in me.

We recorded a song titled "Chasing After" that was inspired by Ecclesiastes 2:1–11. In this chapter, Solomon describes how he set out to find what was worthwhile to pursue in this life. In his searching, he acquired many things, and he filled his life with every kind of pleasure. "I denied myself nothing my eyes desired; I refused my heart no pleasure" (verse 10).

He had everything any man could ever want: laughter,

houses, gardens, gold, beautiful women. He had even become greater by far than any other man in Jerusalem before him. But even after fulfilling every desire he had, somehow he still found himself empty: "Yet when I surveyed all that my hands had done and what I had toiled to achieve, everything was meaningless, a chasing after the wind" (verse 11).

As I read this passage, I found myself reflecting on my own life and the all-too-familiar pain of chasing my own desires and dreams—only to be crushed by my experiences when things didn't work out the way I had planned. I realized that this was not God's design for my life. Relying on my own strength and following blindly after my own desires would only leave me more frustrated and empty than when I first began.

God's plan for my life is so much more than I could ever hope to imagine. The joy found in Him is worth more than anything I could acquire here on earth. Everything else is like "chasing after the wind."

NOTES

WEEK 1

1. Henry T. Blackaby, *Experiencing God Day-By-Day* (Nashville, Tenn.: Broadman & Holman Publishers, 1998), 257.

WEEK 2

2. Point of Grace, *Girls of Grace* (West Monroe, La.: Howard Publishing Co., 2002), 17–18.
3. Ibid., 56.
4. Blackaby, 16.
5. A. W. Tozer, *Tozer on Christian Leadership* (Camp Hill, Pa.: Christian Publications Inc., 2001), March 4.
6. David Jeremiah, *Sanctuary* (Nashville, Tenn.: Integrity Publishers, 2002), 53.
7. Oswald Chambers, *My Utmost for His Highest* (New York: Dodd, Mead & Company, 1935), xx.
8. Chambers, 46.

WEEK 4

9. Jerry Bridges, *The Chase* (Colorado Springs, Colo.: NavPress, 2003), 95.
10. Dr. Leo Buscaglia, *Born for Love* (New York: Random House, 1992), x.
11. Calvin Miller, *The Book of Jesus* (New York: Simon & Schuster, 1996), 171–172.
12. Ibid.
13. Susie Shellenberger, *Brio* magazine, "Taking on a Giant" (Colorado Springs, Colo.: Focus on the Family), Nov. 1997.
14. C. S. Lewis, *Letters to an American Lady* (Grand Rapids, Mich.: William B. Eerdmans Publishing Co., 1967) 109–110.
15. Tim Stafford, Susie Shellenberger and Michael Ross, *Adventures in Singlehood*, (Grand Rapids, Mich.: Zondervan Publishing House, 1996), 93.

WEEK 5

16. Charles H. Spurgeon, *Morning and Evening* (Nashville, Tenn.: Thomas Nelson Publishers, 1994), December 28, evening.

17. Henry T. Blackaby and Claude V. King, *Experiencing God Day-by-Day* (Nashville, Tenn.: Broadman & Holman Publishers, 1998), 242.

18. Camerin Courtney, "A Voice of Racial Harmony," *Today's Christian Woman* magazine, April 2002, 47.

19. Henri Nouwen, *Reaching Out: Three Spiritual Movements* (New York: Doubleday, 1975), 29–30.

20. Anthony DeBarros, "Becoming Christine Dente," *CCM* magazine, October 2003, 53.

21. Dirk R. Buursma, *Daylight Devotional Bible* (Grand Rapids, Mich.: Zondervan Publishing House, 1988), 1328.

22. Max Lucado, *Walking with the Savior* (Wheaton, Ill.: Tyndale House Publishers, 1993), 272.

23. John Eldredge, *Dare to Desire* (Nashville, Tenn.: J. Countryman, 2002), 34

WEEK 6

24. Buursma, 699.

25. Thomas à Kempis *The Imitation of Christ* (San Francisco: HarperCollins Publishers, 2000), 6.

26. Buursma, 1117.

ABOUT THE
AUTHORS

Michael and Tiffany Ross live in Colorado Springs with their son, Christopher, and two cats. Michael is the editor of *Breakaway* magazine and the author of several books for young people, including *Faith That Breathes*. Tiffany is a former production coordinator for Focus on the Family's film department and is now a full-time mom, as well as a student at Fuller Theological Seminary.

Michael and Tiffany love adventure travel. During a trip to Africa, the couple rode motorcycles through Zimbabwe (with a bunch of teens), then took a safari by boat down the Zambezi River.

Notes

Notes

Notes

Notes

If you enjoyed

Faith That Breathes
(for Women)

Also Available from Barbour Publishing. . .

faith that breathes
by michael ross

This unique book uses the real-life stories of contemporary Christian musicians as the basis for six weeks of devotional reading. Features artists such as Toby Mac, Jars of Clay, Third Day, Nicole C. Mullen, and Rebecca St. James.

ISBN 1-59789-240-8
Paperback/336 pages/$4.97